THE FAMILY TREE
CEMETERY
FIELD GUIDE

THE FAMILY TREE
CEMETERY
FIELD GUIDE

HOW TO FIND, RECORD, & PRESERVE
YOUR ANCESTORS' GRAVES

Joy Neighbors

**FAMILY
TREE
BOOKS**

CINCINNATI, OHIO
shopfamilytree.com

CONTENTS

PART
1

PLANNING YOUR TRIP TO THE CEMETERY

Journey to the past! This chapter covers the history and cultural importance
of cemeteries.

Learn what ancestral secrets graveyards hold with this guide to the records
you can find in cemeteries.

Pinpoint graves before even setting foot in the cemetery with this chapter's
guides to online databases like Find A Grave and BillionGraves.

PART
2

RESEARCHING ON HALLOWED GROUND

Maximize your time in the graveyard with these tips for having a successful
cemetery trip, plus a collection of facts to look for while on the ground.

Uncover the family secrets on your ancestor's grave. This chapter discusses
some best practices for reading headstones, including how to safely enhance
inscriptions, overcome weathering, and read old script.

Decipher the words and symbols on your ancestor's grave with this guide to
tombstone symbols.

PART
3

MAKING SENSE OF YOUR RESEARCH

PART
4

DIGGING DEEPER

INTRODUCTION

C emeteries are usually viewed with reservation. Some people see them as a necessity to endure, while others simply avoid them at all costs. Still others hardly give them a thought.

And then there are those of us known as "tombstone tourists." We're the people you see wandering the cemetery grounds armed with notepads, cameras, and, at times, picnic baskets, ready to spend the day in the "silent city." Disrespectful, some may think—but no, far from it. Tombstone tourists are drawn to cemeteries for many reasons: an appreciation for their artwork, the immense history of people and time periods, and the amazing beauty and tranquility awaiting discovery.

We cemetery connoisseurs can rattle off a host of reasons we'd rather visit a graveyard than go to the mall, a circus, or a game. Few other places in the world feature such a stunning array of artwork, architecture, sculpture, stained glass, intricate carvings, and iconography, all providing us with fresh air, exercise, and cultural and historical lessons. And all for free.

Join me as we traverse this hallowed ground searching for ancestors, genealogy records, and a better understanding of who we were and who we have become.

PART ONE

PLANNING YOUR TRIP TO THE CEMETERY

Why Cemeteries?

Cemeteries are repositories for the dead, where we go to seek solace, meditate, and commune with those dearly departed. Graveyards are also sites of historical record, a library of sorts where each stone tells a story and each life was meaningful.

Millions of stones in cemeteries offer glimpses of the people who have gone before us, revealing a spark of humanity in the dead that we only normally see in the living.

A graveyard has an important status in our society—not just as a location to bury our loved ones, but as a place to memorialize, visit, and remember them. It is also a place where we separate, where bonds are broken, where we must let go and finally accept the parting of ways. That is, and always has been, the true essence of a cemetery.

In this chapter, we'll examine the history and cultural importance of cemeteries, plus some of the major types of graveyards.

A HISTORY OF CEMETERIES

We humans have been burying our dead since ancient times as a way of showing respect: a dignified send-off via flame, mummification, burial, or immersion in water. Evidence indicates the Neanderthals first buried their dead fifty thousand years ago in the caves of La Chapelle-aux-Saints in modern France, while other archaeologists claim the practice started as early as one hundred thousand years ago within Mount Precipice/Qafzeh Cave in Israel. Neanderthals were also the first to place flowers in graves with the remains.

The first tomb used for only one individual dates back to 12000 BCE in Israel (containing the remains of a man and his dog), while the Chinese have been credited with making the first coffins (the oldest of which dates back to 5000 BCE and holds the remains of a young girl). The Chinese were also the first to build boat coffins, and the first to use tree trunks as coffins (4000–3000 BCE). The Egyptians developed a process known as mummification for ritualistic purposes around 2600 BCE and began the practice of marking graves with stones bearing the general likeness of the person who had died. The first pyramid—and thus the first documented cemetery marker or monument—was the Step Pyramid constructed for King Zoser at Saqqara in 2750 BCE.

Christian burials began when the Romans excavated burial chambers underground and outside of the city. Christians banded together to form burial societies to ensure that the faithful were interred collectively in a respectful and spiritually appropriate manner. By the third century, several levels of burial chambers existed below ground, and these catacombs became property held in common by the Christian community. Basilicas were built above the catacombs so mass could be said over the graves of the saints and martyrs buried below. Christian burials made directly in the ground that adjoined a church—but could not be interred *in* the church—later became the norm, and some of these churchyards can still be found scattered across the Christian world.

Across the Atlantic in North America, the Clovis people, early mammoth hunters, practiced respectful burial of their dead more than twelve thousand years ago. The grave of a twelve-to-eighteen-month-old boy was discovered in 1968 in Montana. The young child's remains were covered with powdered red ochre (a sign of respect and ritual) and surrounded by 125 artifacts, including dozens of spear points and antler tools, to aid him on his journey into the afterlife.

With the advancements of the Industrial Revolution during the eighteenth and nineteenth centuries, people began to be buried farther away from home. Large city cemeteries formed and quickly filled up, and cemeteries dealt with this overcrowding by allowing a body to rest in a grave for a set amount of years (or sometimes months) before digging up the remains and reusing the plot for someone else. (The excavated remains were then tossed into a communal burial pit located elsewhere on the grounds.) Another option was to rebury the remains deeper in the earth and then bury on top of them. These methods were especially useful in paupers' cemeteries of the nineteenth century. Today, lack of sufficient burial space is again creating a dilemma, and many of the suggestions being considered harken back to remedies from the 1700 and 1800s.

It's impossible to say where and when the first cemetery in the United States was founded, since hundreds of tiny burial grounds were created when settlers needed to bury family members. Cemeteries and graveyards of the seventeenth and eighteenth centuries, while more organized, were not welcoming places. Death was an accepted part of life in the Old World, but death was feared, dreaded, and mourned in the New World.

The early Puritans believed in sparse burials with little to no decoration. Most stones bore only a brief inscription, usually the person's name and the date of death. The only decoration on these early graves was rather morbid. A common symbol was the winged death's-head figure: a winged skull with crossed bones symbolizing the religious belief that death brought eternal life. Each community had its stylized version of the death's-head, based on how its religious leaders and stonecarvers thought it should look. During this time, a stylized hourglass with wings could also be found on gravestones, symbolizing the flight of time for the mortal soul. Death would later be depicted as a skeletal man with a scythe: "The Grim Reaper," the harvester of souls (image **A**).

Image A: The Grim Reaper "harvests" souls and brings them to the afterlife.

During the late 1700s, Colonial New England began to loosen its harsh orthodox religious views, and gravestones started to show more uplifting images of cherubs and angels, although the death's-head continued to be used in and around Boston. By the 1790s and early 1800s, willow trees (image **B**) and floral motifs began to decorate tombstones, providing a less morbid outlook toward death, and instead focusing on more positive natural images. This was also the age of portrait stones, where a general likeness of the deceased's stoic face was carved upon his marker (image **C**).

With the arrival of the nineteenth century, attitudes about death began to change. Mourning became popular and death became more mysterious. In 1831, Mount Auburn Cemetery in Cambridge, Massachusetts, was considered the epitome of what an American cemetery could and should be. This original "rural" or "garden" cemetery was landscaped to make it appear more park-like. Inspired by the English garden city movement, the rural cemetery was composed of acres of rolling hills and pastoral settings, featuring lakes, walking paths, wooded

Image B: Weeping willows and other floral patterns were used to make tombstones less morbid.

Image C: Some tombstones include depictions of the deceased.

groves, and other landscape designs that made the cemetery feel tranquil and welcoming. This was a place to "take the air," a genteel way to see and be seen. It was a chance to escape from the dirt and noise of the city for a few hours and enjoy a contemplative stroll among exquisite sculpture, interesting architecture, and acres of rolling hills and valleys.

The rural cemetery was also something of a democratic ideal. Anyone—regardless of religion, ethnicity, or economic class—could stroll its grounds or purchase a burial plot. This wrestled control away from churches, which could punish people by refusing them a burial plot based on their religious affiliation or moral character (or supposed lack thereof).

A rural cemetery was not just a place in the countryside to bury your dead; it was an attraction that appealed to those nineteenth-century traits of nostalgia, melancholy, and romance. The concept became so popular that by 1836, seven more rural cemeteries were being created in the eastern United States, including Laurel Hill Cemetery in Philadelphia and Green-Wood Cemetery in Brooklyn. By the mid-1850s, another batch of rural cemeteries had been developed in Midwestern and southern states, including Spring Grove Cemetery in Cincinnati, Allegheny Cemetery in Pittsburgh, and Elmwood Cemetery in Detroit.

The appearance of the rural cemetery was quite timely, since the Victorian Era also ushered in death as a full-blown business, complete with special mourning clothes, burial superstitions, funeral etiquette, and death mementos. Thanks to Queen Victoria and the forty years she spent grieving for her husband Prince Albert, Victorians embraced death and mourning with numerous rules of etiquette in order to avoid exhibiting poor taste. For example, Victorians were required to mourn for a set period of time. A widow was expected to be in mourning clothes, or "widow's weeds," for at least two years after the demise of a husband, although many dressed in black for the remainder of their lives. A widower, on the other hand, was only required to be in mourning for one year.

Rural cemeteries featured beautiful properties, with amazing architecture, stunning sculpture, and gorgeous park-like settings where families could enjoy picnicking, visiting, and concerts. They became virtual outdoor museums filled with sculpture, stained glass, and carvings by the most popular artists and craftsmen of the time: Louis Comfort Tiffany, Giulio Monteverde, and Auguste Rodin, to name a few. Stones and monuments became more artistic, grander, and more momentous.

Image D: Mausoleums became standard-issue for the wealthy in the 1800s.

Image E: This grieving woman atop a grave holds a wreath, symbolizing victory over death.

Image F: Lambs appearing on a tombstone usually indicated the death of a child.

Mausoleums became de rigueur for the rich (image **D**), and obelisks marked the graves of those who had been up-and-coming in the community. (While flouting wealth would be considered crass beyond the cemetery gates, wealthy members of society could strut their status here without fear of social stigma.)

In our modern world, many people prefer to avoid the cemetery, afraid of the unknown or dreading their own eventual mortality—or, for the more superstitious, spooked by spirits. Gone is that Victorian sense of history and random beauty. Today, our cemeteries are laid out in perfect rows with standardized markers made of certain materials, crafted in certain shapes, and bearing certain designs; almost all are mass-produced. Our creativity toward death has been stifled. Cemeteries of the twenty-first century are less inviting and less interesting than those from the mid-1800s through the mid-1900s, a period that took the time to tell a story about the person buried below the marker: a woman mourning the loss of her loved one atop a monument (image **E**), or young lambs snuggled together as a reminder that death can claim even the young (image **F**).

TYPES OF CEMETERIES

A cemetery can consist of a few family graves in a tiny burial plot or thousands of graves scattered across acres of prime real estate. But regardless of a cemetery's size, family researchers and tombstone tourists still need to understand how different kinds of cemeteries are set up and where to go to find elusive burial forms.

There are six main types of cemeteries to consider when searching for an ancestor's burial location and records, and identifying what kind of cemetery your ancestors are buried in makes it easier to locate. If you have a problem finding a cemetery, check with the local genealogical or historical society. These groups are great resources for local data since they work to preserve valuable information like burial indexes and can connect you with community members who may be able to assist researchers in locating little-known, or forgotten graveyards.

Churchyards and Graveyards

Although we use the terms interchangeably today, "churchyard" and "graveyard" originally had different meanings. A churchyard was exactly that: a piece of consecrated ground that surrounded or was adjacent to a church. A graveyard, meanwhile, was any land set aside for burying the dead.

Religious burial grounds are some of the oldest organized cemeteries, dating back to the Middle Ages. Churchyard burial grounds were usually small and never had enough space to bury the current generation of members. Over time, bodies were dug up and placed in community burial pits, while new bodies were interred in the current graves. Unfortunately, this led to diseases being spread through contact with the remains—just one reason bodies began to be buried six feet deep.

These hallowed grounds were available for church members only. The charge for a burial varied, depending on the churchyard. Some churches buried members for free or for a nominal fee, while others would charge more in order to maintain the graves and the grounds. Many churches request a burial fee, but then offer members some financial support so they could afford the burial. Graves located outside

Breathing Life into Stones: Louis Baker

Even one's final day could be preserved in stone, as the monument to Louis Baker proves.

At the turn of the twentieth century, Baker was a stonecarver in the tiny town of Bedford, Indiana, when a spring storm rolled in as he finished his work day. Believing he could beat the storm—or possibly being cavalier in his youth—Baker set out down the road toward home. The next morning, he was not at his workbench. No one had heard from him since 5 p.m. the night before. Baker was found lying by the road, near his home, struck dead by a bolt of lighting.

His fellow stonecarvers decided to honor him in the only way they knew how: They recreated Baker's workbench in limestone, with scattered tools, tossed apron, and in-progress limestone slabs as they were just before he went out into that fateful spring storm.

Some tombstones use elaborate symbols, such as these carvings of objects from a stonecarver's shop, to tell the deceased's story.

the cemetery fence or wall were set aside for those souls who were unwanted by the church—stillborns, bastards, slaves, or people who had committed suicide, or those who were simply unknown.

Church cemeteries were governed by laws and a board of directors. If a church experienced a loss due to some act of nature (or God, as the case may be)—or if it had to rebuild in a different location for other reasons—the old cemetery might become untended and abandoned over the years. If so, a regional government entity could take it over.

Also, as the population of villages and towns grew, real estate values increased. Property like this was then purchased for development, but the previous owners didn't always move the cemetery's contents to another location. Sometimes the remains were relocated, other times only the markers were moved, and many times stones were pulled up and another structure was built over the existing graves with no indication that the land had once been a cemetery. (Who knows how many subdivisions currently sit on top of former cemeteries?)

Clergy should be able to assist you in gaining access to churchyard records and deeds. If you are not able to locate your ancestor's records at the local level, religious communities have statewide and national offices where burial and membership information may be archived. Contact them for assistance, or for more guidance.

Public and Municipal Cemeteries

A public cemetery (image **G**) is owned and controlled by a government entity, usually a city, town, village, county, or township where the land is located. State and national jurisdictions maintain burial facilities for veterans and their families. If someone who was destitute dies, a public cemetery will bury the deceased without charge, as part of their responsibility to the community.

By law, a municipal cemetery must remain open to everyone because it's funded by tax dollars, which are collected from the public and used to maintain the grounds for the benefit of the people. This also means local government employees can use city or county equipment for the use, upkeep, and maintenance of the grounds. Cemeteries with

Image G: Public cemeteries allow people of any faith tradition to be buried, and the local government is in charge of the cemetery's maintenance and recordkeeping.

graves more than fifty years old may also be eligible to receive funds for historic preservation that could assist in their upkeep.

Since a public cemetery accepts anyone, grave markers can vary from small poured concrete stones to large ornate monuments and mausoleums. This is what makes public cemeteries some of the most visually fascinating burial grounds to explore.

Private Cemeteries

Private cemeteries are just that: private. They are not owned by a government entity, but by private organizations, corporations, fraternal lodges, or individuals.

A private cemetery can be for-profit or not-for-profit. A for-profit status affects the cost and upkeep at the cemetery, making it a more expensive burial option than a public cemetery, something to keep in mind if your ancestors had money and would have preferred to be buried "among their own class."

Owners or caretakers of private burial grounds may be listed at the cemetery entrance on a sign or plaque located near the gate, sometimes with their phone numbers or other contact info. You'll need this information if you're seeking admittance to the cemetery—remember, this land is just as private as someone's home. You should gain permission to search the grounds of a private cemetery, or you will be trespassing.

To locate the owner of a private cemetery, visit the office of the county assessor, land surveyor, or county recorder to find land ownership maps. If a cemetery was once private and is no longer being used or maintained, the local government may have taken it over, and you may no longer need to gain permission to access it. Also, check with local and regional historical societies to see if any of their members can identify who owns the cemetery.

Family and Customary Cemeteries

Family cemeteries were located on the homestead and set aside for the burial of specific family members. A customary cemetery, meanwhile, might also include the remains of close friends and neighbors (something to keep in mind if you can't find an ancestor in the local public cemetery). The customary burial ground had no legal status and was usually tended by the descendants of those buried there.

Many family and customary cemeteries have been in use since the land was first settled, and these burial grounds can be found in rural settings, on family farms, or outside small communities. Whether any records or formal papers still exist—if they ever did—is questionable.

GRAVE TIP

Go International: Ancestors who died while in service overseas may be buried in one of twenty-four American cemeteries located outside of the country, all of which are administered by the American Battle Monuments Commission. During World War I, 40 percent of US soldiers who died overseas were buried in eight permanent American cemeteries scattered throughout Europe. In World War II, fourteen permanent US cemeteries in Europe were created for our military dead.

At one time, there were thousands of family burial places, but more are being abandoned to nature each year.

Family and customary graveyards usually contain the most personal family information, but their usefulness to researchers is offset by their difficulty to locate. If you're having difficulty finding a family graveyard, it might be worth searching through family Bibles and personal papers for maps or notations kept on the burials. In these cemeteries, you may discover what happened to children in the family, many of whom died young due to illness, birth complications, or accidents, all of which could be listed on tombstones.

Once these tiny graveyards were left untended for a long period of time, the town or county could annex the land and sell it, which is why so many small family cemeteries have literally vanished off the map. Although family burial grounds are still legal in most states, few are being developed today due to governmental rules and regulations related to human remains and cemetery maintenance, a public health and welfare issue. Today, such cemeteries are usually cared for by the current landowner or the local historical society, but rarely by the original family's descendants.

If the local genealogical or historical society can't help locate a family cemetery, check with regional funeral homes. A cemetery may have changed names over the years, or the regional dialect may affect the way you're hearing the name said. Local funeral homes know where many lost or forgotten burial grounds are, even though burials no longer occur there.

Fraternal and Lodge Cemeteries

A fraternal cemetery (image **H**) is owned by an organization that has banded together as a group to uphold certain traditions and maintain appointed codes of conduct. The group may be religious, chivalric, social, cultural, mutually beneficial, or charitable. Examples of fraternal and lodge cemeteries include the Independent Order of Odd Fellows, the Benevolent and Protective Order of Elks, the Modern Woodmen of America (MWA), the Woodmen of the World, and the Freemasons.

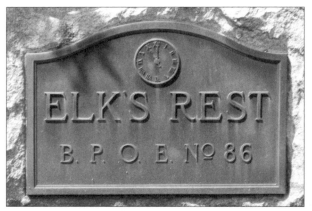

Image H: Some cemeteries serve members of particular fraternal organizations, such as this one for the Elks.

Lodge cemeteries may restrict interment to only include members (and sometimes their families.)

Many fraternal organizations were founded to provide burial insurance for their members. For example, the MWA is a fraternal benefit society founded to financially protect its members and their families in the event of the sole provider's death. We'll talk more about fraternal organizations like the MWA in chapters 6 and 9.

Fraternal burial grounds can be located within public or private cemeteries or on land owned by the group. A part of the organization's membership dues goes toward the upkeep and maintenance of the cemetery. Records for these groups are still kept at state and national fraternal headquarters.

If you're having trouble locating detailed information about an organization, consider that many fraternal groups published books that explain their histories and depict anniversary celebrations. Your ancestor may be listed in the attendance rolls or even appear in a photograph. If the organization proves to be difficult to find any information on, check the Encyclopedia of Associations **<find.galegroup.com/gdl/ help/GDLeDirEAHelp.html>**, which contains information on more than twenty thousand societies and associations that have existed in the United States.

While your grandfather may have belonged to the local fraternal organization, once the lodge relocated or closed, those records were probably sent to the state association, or directly to the national headquarters. If the fraternal group has ceased to exist, check with state historical societies, or contact the state where the main headquarters was located to discover if the records were preserved there. Keep in mind that in our twenty-first-century world, confidentiality is paramount, so you may have to offer some proof of your relationship to a member before an organization will send any requested information to you. Also, remember that these groups are not in the family history business. They are private organizations and may decline to provide any information—disappointing to the family genealogist, but their decision to make.

Military and Veterans' Cemeteries

The US government operates military and veterans' burial grounds as part of the National Cemetery Administration (NCA), which was created during the Civil War. The Army's burial system was found to be inadequate to keep up with the large number of soldiers dying during the Civil War. In 1862, Congress approved legislation authorizing President Abraham Lincoln to purchase ground in several states to be used as national cemeteries "for soldiers who shall have died in the service of the country."

Cemeteries for Confederate soldiers were not designated as such until Resaca Confederate Cemetery was established in October 1866 in Resaca, Georgia. During the war, Confederate troops were either buried where they fell, or (if the Southern line was close enough) an undertaker under contract with the Confederate government would attempt to get the bodies back across the Southern line to be buried in Southern soil.

One of the first military cemeteries, and also one of the largest, is Arlington National Cemetery in Arlington County, Virginia, the resting place of more than four hundred thousand American veterans and their families (image I). Currently, more than three thousand ceremonies take place in Arlington each year.

The Mystery of My Great-Grandparents' Graves

When my great-grandmother died, I was traumatized. It was my first brush with death as a child. All I remember is the funeral, a lone, windswept hill, and the name of the burial ground: Beetle Cemetery. When I began searching for her grave forty years later, I ran into a series of dead-ends: There was no Beetle Cemetery in the county where she died.

After several attempts, I contacted local funeral homes and found the one that had handled her arrangements. Filed in their records was an original memorial card for my great-grandmother's funeral. Listed on the card was "Interment in Biddle Cemetery." *Biddle*, not Beetle.

Promising, but after more phone calls and visits to the local genealogical society, I discovered that there was no cemetery by this name in the county. After some in-depth sleuthing at the historical library, I found an old book with a list of all the cemeteries in the county and surrounding counties—and that's where I found it: *Bedell* Cemetery, in an adjacent county.

After doing some research, I discovered that my great-grandmother, who died when I was young, was buried in *Bedell* Cemetery, not *Beetle* Cemetery.

My great-grandmother, Rachel France, was buried near another set of my great-grandparents. How did they know each other? The tombstone's placement in the cemetery raises new questions for me to research.

Following the hand-drawn map sketched by a member of the society, I traversed country roads until I began to recognize the area, then I crested the final hill into the cemetery.

Upon entering the small graveyard, I walked directly to my maternal great-grandmother's grave. I had found her! But along with my great-grandmother, there were also plots for my great-grandfather and a son of theirs whom I had never heard about. Here were three of my relatives buried in this remote country family cemetery with no known ties to us. (The research was getting interesting!)

But that wasn't all. In walking the small grounds, I also located the "missing" grave of my paternal great-grandparents. I was not aware that the families had known each other well. But here they were, buried in the same Bedell family cemetery, catty-cornered from one another—but why here?

The rest of the families were buried in local cemeteries, the maternal members laid to rest in cemeteries within a few miles of each other. Paternal members were mainly buried in the local cemetery back in town, so now I have more research to do to answer these questions: What led to not one but two sets of great-grandparents being buried there? How did they receive these plots? What's the connection?

This is what makes family history so much fun (and, at times, so frustrating) to explore.

1

Image I: Military and veterans' cemeteries honor the men and women who served in the armed forces.

Military cemeteries provide a free burial for veterans and their spouses, and that includes the burial plot and headstone. There are currently 149 military cemeteries in the United States, some located in local cemeteries on sections of land set aside for veterans and managed by the NCA. Today, more than 22 million veterans have earned the honor of being buried in a national military cemetery. This is just one way our country remembers and pays tribute to our veterans' service, sacrifice, and valor.

It is interesting to note, though, that the majority of veterans are buried in local or private cemeteries in the area where they lived, sometimes in sections that have been reserved for veterans of the community.

 ## KEYS from the CRYPT

• Learn the burial customs and practices of your ancestor's time. These can help you learn more about your ancestor and his culture and beliefs, plus give you clues about where to search for his grave (and what kind of symbols to search for).

• Contact local archives and historical and genealogical societies to learn about the history and cemeteries of a region.

• Determine which kind of cemetery your ancestor is buried in, as this will affect your ability to access records.

2

Cemetery Records Crash Course

emetery records offer a wealth of information for the genealogist and family historian. These burial records have been kept in some organized form since the mid-1800s, and church graveyards have kept track of their burials for much longer. These documents contain tidbits of vital information you won't learn from other sources: a grave for a child who was never acknowledged, or an "extra" wife who was never spoken of. These little surprises can assist you in learning more about the deceased, their deaths, and their lives.

Image A: Cemeteries contain a host of records that you can apply to your research.

While you may only think about grave transcriptions (i.e., the carvings on grave markers), cemeteries contain several types of files that can reveal information about your departed ancestors, including sexton's records, cemetery deeds, plot records, plat maps, and burial permits (image **A**).

Regardless of format and purpose, most cemetery documents contain the same or similar information: names, death dates, burial dates, plot locations, etc. But some forms may contain extra details—tidbits that can help you learn more about the deceased. Discovering the name of the informant who provided the final information for your deceased ancestor, and his relationship to the deceased, may introduce you to a new member of your family tree.

In this chapter, we'll discuss each of the major kinds of cemetery records and what you can reasonably expect to find in each.

SEXTON'S RECORDS/RECORDS OF INTERMENT

Also known as records of interment, the registry of burials, and "cemetery books," sexton's records are documents kept in the cemetery office. Today, all public cemeteries have superintendents and offices with certain hours of operation, or at least a phone number to call for assistance. Note these records are not necessarily written in a book and may be contained in ledgers or notebooks, on loose papers in filing cabinets, or even on index cards kept in boxes.

Older cemetery books (image **B**) contain three basic types of records: chronological records of burials, reports pertaining to where the graves are located, and cemetery deeds (see the next section). Burial records include the name of the person buried and the date of burial, but additional details (such as the name of the plot owner or how much was paid for the plot) will vary based on the sexton. Cemetery files may also include information on plots not sold, plus exact measurements of the lot.

Look for records online at DeathIndexes.com <**www.deathindexes. com**>, where you can search for obituaries, indexes, records, and cemeteries by state.

Image B: Old cemetery books and ledgers contain a wealth of information.

CEMETERY DEEDS

A cemetery deed, like any deed, is issued for the purchase of land, albeit a piece of real estate just large enough to bury the dead. The original deed is given to the purchaser, and the cemetery office keeps a copy for its files (image **C**). As with any other parcel of land, any transfer, sale, or inheritance involving this deed is recorded by the cemetery and the city or county recorder of deeds office where the cemetery is located. The deed includes the size and dimensions of the plot, name and address of the buyer and seller, amount paid, location of the burial lot (including section and plot number), and the name and address of the cemetery where the plot is located. By researching the cemetery deed, you might discover other plots that were also sold to the same buyer, dates of the purchase, how much was paid, if the plots were ever used, and who was buried there.

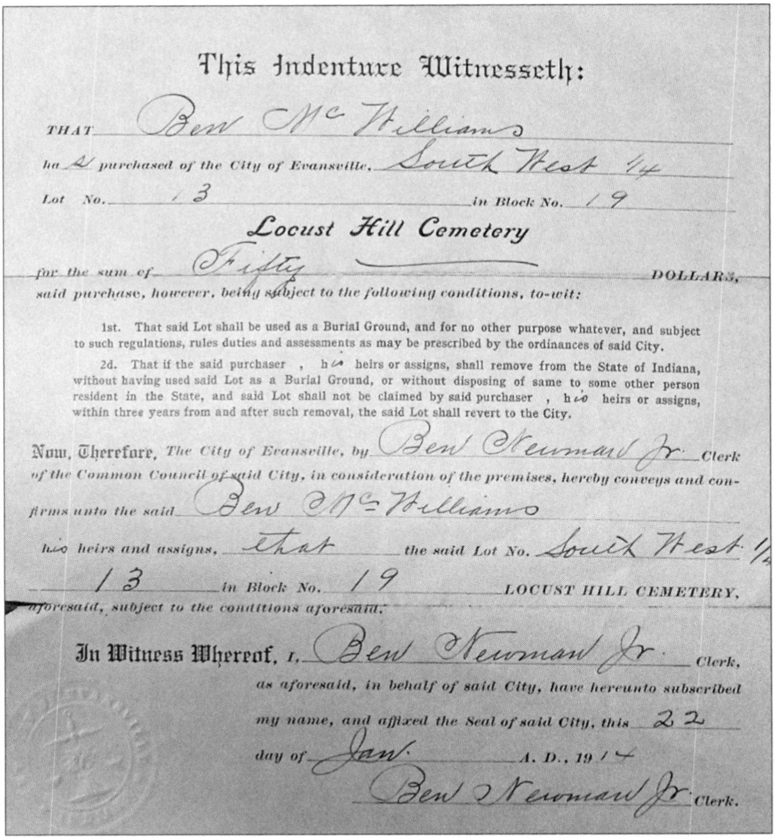

This Indenture Witnesseth:

THAT Ben McWilliams

has purchased of the City of Evansville, South West 1/4

Lot No. 13 in Block No. 19

Locust Hill Cemetery

for the sum of Fifty DOLLARS,

said purchase, however, being subject to the following conditions, to-wit:

1st. That said Lot shall be used as a Burial Ground, and for no other purpose whatever, and subject to such regulations, rules duties and assessments as may be prescribed by the ordinances of said City.

2d. That if the said purchaser , his heirs or assigns, shall remove from the State of Indiana, without having used said Lot as a Burial Ground, or without disposing of same to some other person resident in the State, and said Lot shall not be claimed by said purchaser , his heirs or assigns, within three years from and after such removal, the said Lot shall revert to the City.

Now, Therefore, The City of Evansville, by Ben Newman Jr. Clerk of the Common Council of said City, in consideration of the premises, hereby conveys and confirms unto the said Ben McWilliams his heirs and assigns, that the said Lot No. South West 1/4 13 in Block No. 19 LOCUST HILL CEMETERY, aforesaid, subject to the conditions aforesaid.

In Witness Whereof, I, Ben Newman Jr. Clerk, as aforesaid, in behalf of said City, have hereunto subscribed my name, and affixed the Seal of said City, this 22 day of Jan. A. D., 1914

Ben Newman Jr. Clerk.

Image C: Cemetery deeds recorded the transfer of burial plots between people, giving you some information about your ancestors (often while they were still alive).

PLOT RECORDS AND PLAT MAPS

Before local governments became involved in overseeing cemeteries, no one put too much thought into diagramming or mapping out burial grounds. Those who died were usually buried in order of demise, grouped together as families, or buried wherever it was convenient. This can make it a challenge to locate graves in an older cemetery: There may be a record of who was buried where, but without an original plat map, the actual location of the grave may be lost to time. A visit to the cemetery's office or a local genealogical society could provide you with the original plot records and/or plat maps.

Plot records contain information about the physical grave lot, usually the location or section, the plot or grave number, and a visual description of the site. You may also find the deed number, who the deed was issued to, when the plot was purchased, how much was paid, and if other plots were purchased at the same time. Plot records can be found in a "lot book." These records will often include a description of the grave monument, including inscriptions and symbols.

Plat maps (image **D**) are just that: maps that show the layout of all the graves in the cemetery. The plat book includes the burial section

GRAVE TIP

Leave a Trail: Ask the cemetery superintendent if you can leave an index card in your ancestor's file that has your name, address, e-mail address, phone number, and relationship to the deceased. This will allow others researching this person to connect with you, opening the door for future research collaboration.

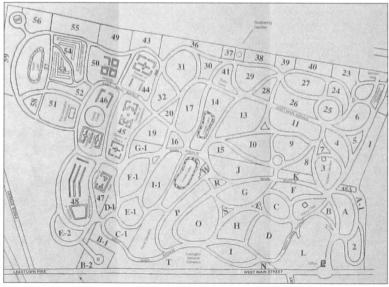

Image D: Plat maps show you where individual tracts of land are within a cemetery.

name and location number, the burial row number, and the grave or plot number. Additional details like who owns the grave and possible deed information may also be included. (These records can contain redundant information, but a change in one number or one letter can send you off on a new research adventure, so always pay attention and make sure the numbers correlate.)

Once you have found an ancestor's grave on a plat map, pay attention to the names on the stones nearby. These could be family members, in-laws, close friends, or neighbors. Compare your findings to census records and see where these names fit into the scheme of things. Also, keep a list of the names to refer back to when you hit that inevitable brick wall.

Let's look at a couple examples to see what plot maps can tell us about our ancestors, and to see what doors they can open in our research. Plot maps are interesting in that they show the arrangement of burials in a family plot and how the cemetery ensured that everyone had adequate space. Notice the family plot in image **E** was sold to William Bedford, Sr., for $12.50. The location is in section two, lot number four. Notice, too, that burials 10 through 12A also reference what type of burial container was used: a concrete vault, concrete box, cremation vault, or concrete cremation vault. On June 27, 1942, someone paid $150 for "endowment care" for this plot, meaning regular maintenance and care of the plot (such as grass cutting and trimming, plant and tree care, road upkeep, and drainage of the cemetery).

So what can we learn about the deceased? We see thirteen people were buried here, but not in a row as you might think. Anna Bedford was laid to rest first in the corner plot, followed by William Isley who was buried catty-cornered to Anna. William Bedford, the purchaser, was then buried next to the family monument (*MON*). As you read down the list, you can also see where the graves were placed and who was buried next to whom. Knowing the family genealogy can tell us which of these women was William's wife and which were daughters or daughters-in-law. The name *Meadows* appears on four graves, and *Norcross* is listed on one. What was the relationship between these people, since all are interred in the Bedford family plot? The burial plot opens new lines of questions in your research.

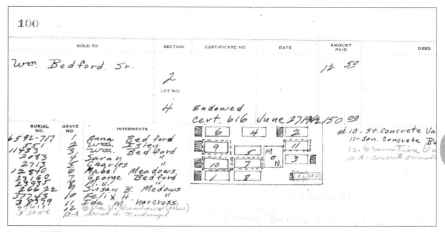

Image E: This detailed plot record for the Bradford family plot provides valuable information, but also raises new research questions.

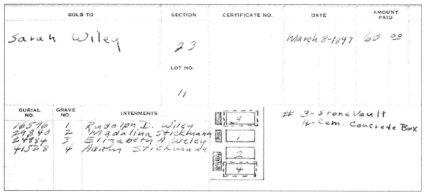

Image F: Sarah Wiley purchased this four-grave burial lot, but she wasn't buried in it. So who are the people who were buried there, and how are they related to her?

In the next example (image **F**), Sarah Wiley purchased section 23 and lot number 11 for $60 on March 8, 1897, a spot large enough for four graves. Since Sarah bought the plot and her husband, Rudolph, is the first to be buried there, we can reasonably guess that her husband Rudolph's death made buying a burial plot for the family necessary. The second to be laid to rest here was a woman named Madalina Stickmann. Could this be Sarah's mother? Elizabeth Weley (notice the spelling change?) was the third to be buried in the plot, and she was placed next to Rudolph—possibly a daughter—followed by an Adam Stickmann, next to Madalina. But Sarah herself was not interred here.

Now we have unanswered questions. If Sarah were Rudolph's wife, did she remarry? Was she buried with her next husband? Or was Elizabeth the wife, since she is resting next to Rudolph? This seems unlikely as, at that time, a woman would have been able to purchase a plot for her husband, but probably not a daughter. If she were married, her

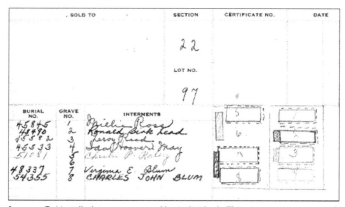

Image G: Not all plots were owned by individuals. This one was a communal plot in which individuals were buried as needed. Note lot number 6 is empty.

husband would have made the purchase for her. If she were too young to be married, a brother or uncle would have made the plot purchase. There are definitely plenty of questions that need answering, thanks to this plot listing.

One final example shows a communal plot (image **G**). Notice that most of the last names vary, and each person is buried in death order. This indicates these graves were sold independently, as needed. A listing to the side (not pictured) also tells us what type of container each person was buried in. Interestingly, lot number six was never filled; there is a double headstone—which indicates that Christina P. Roley's spouse intended to be buried next to her but never was. Another clue to investigate in someone's family tree.

BURIAL PERMITS AND RECORDS

Burial permits, known today as "disposition of remains" permits, are government documents allowing a body to be buried. They're granted by a state's local board of health or the town clerk in the town where the death occurred (even if the body is to be buried in another town). State and city health departments have been regulating burials since the beginning of the twentieth century.

A burial permit is issued to a funeral director or embalmer who is registered with the local board of health. The permit is then filled out by the funeral home handling the arrangements. A death certificate may be required to accompany the permit. Burial permits always include the name of the deceased and the date of death, but may also be issued as burial/removal permits that allow for the removal of the remains from the funeral home so they may be transported to the cemetery to be interred.

These permits can be as simple or as detailed as the department that issued them desired. A burial permit may also include the city in which the death occurred (not necessarily where the deceased had actually lived), the burial date, section and plot numbers in the cemetery, the name of the informant who provided information about the deceased, and that person's relationship to the deceased. A burial

Physicians are reminded of the importance of filling out these Certificates with accuracy.   They are the basis of the Mortuary Statistics of the City.

BURIAL CERTIFICATE.

ST. LOUIS.

No. _4968_

This Certificate must be fully and accurately filled out, as provided by Ordinance 10,329, approved July 17, 1877.

Name of Deceased _Chas Yegty_

Age, _1_ Years, _8_ Months, Days.

Male.   White.   Single.   } Cross out the words not required.
Female. Colored. Married.
                   Widowed.

Occupation _____

Place of Birth, _St. Louis_   Length of Residence in St. Louis, _20 Months_

Place of Death, No. _7 Fayer_

Exact Locality { Block.   { North by _____ St. East by _____ St.
of Death.   { BOUNDED. { West by _____ St. South by _____ St.

City Ward No. _____

Date of Death   _July 20 —_

Cause of Death*   _Merin. ptis_

I CERTIFY that I attended the person above named in _hi_ last illness, who died of the disease stated, on the date above named.

C. A. Ware M. D.

Address _217 N 14 t_

Place of Burial   _Evansville Indiana_

N. S. Clement Undertaker.

OFFICE HEALTH DEPARTMENT,

St. Louis, Mo. _July 21_ _____ 188_1_

I CERTIFY that I have examined this Certificate, and find it to accord with the requirements of the City Ordinances and Charter.

Health Commissioner.

Clerk of Health Commissioner and Board of Health.

Sextons receiving Burial Certificates without the signature of the Commissioner or his Clerk, will subject themselves to a fine, as provided by Ordinance 10,329.

*In filling out the above Certificate, Physicians are earnestly requested to conform strictly to the Nomenclature printed on the back.

IF THIS CERTIFICATE IS NOT PROPERLY FILLED OUT, IT WILL NOT BE RECEIVED OR SIGNED.

Image H: Burial certificates can provide tons of information about your ancestors: age, date and place of birth and death, cause of death, and more.

permit will also sometimes list the manner of death, be it natural causes, accident, homicide, suicide, or undetermined circumstances (as well as if there is a pending investigation into the cause). The burial permit stays in the possession of the funeral director until after the burial has been completed.

Other records that are sometimes listed with a burial permit include burial transit permits, grave opening and closing orders, and information on disinterment of remains. In addition, our children and grandchildren will benefit from additional burial forms to use when researching more-recent burials: funeral order forms, on hold grave forms, and pinning forms.

Let's look at a couple of examples to learn what burial certificates can teach us. The St. Louis burial certificate for Charles Negley (image **H**) indicates he was one year, eight months old when he died. We also learn he was a white male who was born and died in St. Louis, although the exact place of death is hard to decipher. Charles died on July 20, 1881, of meningitis. Notice that he was buried in Evansville, Indiana, by an undertaker named W. S. Clement. Looking for files from Mr. Clement may help unravel why young Charles was buried more than 160 miles from his birthplace.

The burial certificate for Lizzie R. Utteridge (image **I**) was originally hard to read, but I can make out a little more by manipulating the image in iPhoto. I heighten the contrast to decipher more words, which lets me see Lizzie was born in Indiana and died at the age of four months on July 21, 1881, in Warrick County, Indiana. Her parent's religion was Cumberland Presbyterian, which led me to research church records from that congregation. I found a website <**www.cumberland.org/hfcpc**> that hosts digitized Presbyterian records, and here I learned Lizzie's cause of death was "cholera infantum" and "congestions of the brain."

By researching the two causes, we learn more about her death. Children in the United States were very susceptible to "cholera infantum," a gastrointestinal illness that caused fever, vomiting, and diarrhea (Note: This is a separate, often deadly disease from cholera, a highly contagious disease that often manifested in outbreaks throughout the nineteenth century). At the time, the doctors believed this "summer

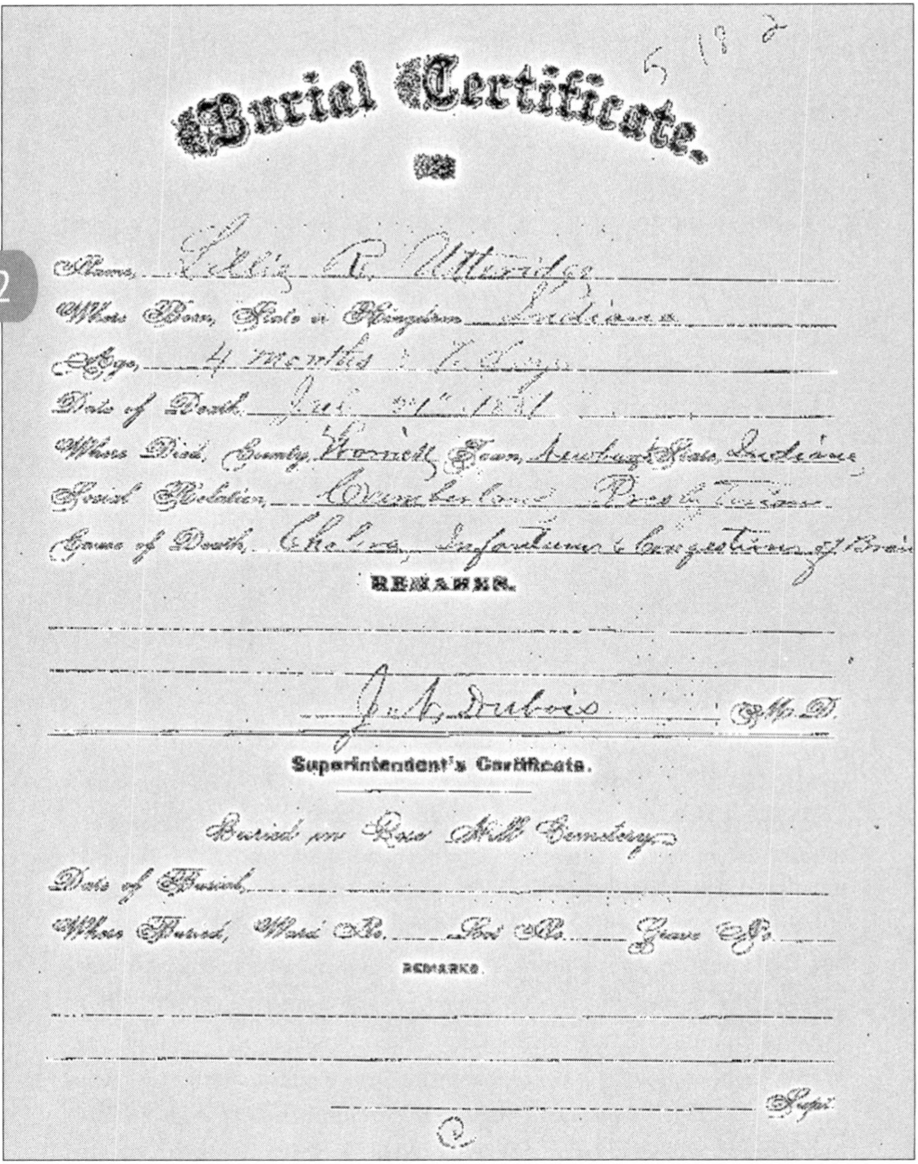

Burial Certificate.

Name, Lillie R. Utteridge

Where Born, State or Kingdom Indiana

Age, 4 months & 7 days

Date of Death Jul. 27th 1881

Where Died, County Warrick Town Newburgh State Indiana

Social Relation, Cumberland Presbyterian

Cause of Death, Cholera Infantum & Congestion of Brain

REMARKS.

J. A. Dubois M. D.

Superintendent's Certificate.

Buried in Rose Hill Cemetery

Date of Burial

Where Buried, Ward No. Lot No. Grave No.

REMARKS.

Supt.

Image I: Not all records will be easy to read, but you can overcome this by scanning documents, then manipulating the images in photoediting programs. Consult other sources for even more insight.

complaint" (as it was sometimes called) to be caused by teething or hot weather, but it was more likely due to eating food that had gone bad.

"Congestion of the brain," meanwhile, occurred when blood accumulated in the brain, possibly due to an infection. The brain would swell cutting off arterial flow to other parts, which could cause sudden death. Treatment at that time was to divert blood from the head by administering hot mustard footbaths, and by applying ice or cold water to the head (probably, in a cruel irony, the same water that could cause cholera).

At the end of the burial certificate, we see that Lizzie was buried in Rose Hill Cemetery in Evansville, Indiana, but the date of burial was not listed. While Rose Hill records are not plentiful, a walk in the cemetery may reveal not only Lizzie's grave but also those of other family members, possibly names we didn't know. And the search goes on ...

FUNERAL RECORD FORMS

Cemetery papers may also include funeral record (or funeral service) forms, created by the undertaker to glean pertinent information about the deceased's burial.

In this example, the funeral record is for John Williams (image **J**) provides a lot of information to the family genealogist. From the record, we see that his daughter ordered the funeral after his death from tuberculosis. We also learn Mr. William was a retired merchant

Costs That Kill

Funeral and burial services have never been free, and the cost of memorializing the deceased has increased dramatically throughout the years. In 1898, opening a grave cost five dollars, while the grand total for a retired businessman's middle class funeral was ninety-nine dollars—about three thousand dollars today, and still a bargain. Modern funerals, by comparison, can cost anywhere from eight to eleven thousand dollars.

Image J: Funeral record forms were used as reference material for undertakers and can be valuable to researchers today.

Pay a Visit: If the cemetery you're searching has no office, check with the folks at city hall. There's usually a department that oversees local or county cemeteries, and a map of burials may be kept there. If not, visit the local genealogical or historical society and talk with area historians. A local library may also have books that pertain to burials in the region.

and a widower, and his parents were German and he was raised in the Catholic faith. The funeral service was to take place at 8 AM and would feature six pallbearers. The record even describes his casket: adorned with a cross and having six handles, along with a plate that read "Our Father." He was laid to rest in a burial robe in St. Joseph's Cemetery, and the record provides the lot number and section number given. Notice that seven carriages were hired to transport the funeral guests to the cemetery.

Today we have "grave opening and closing orders" that allow for the digging and filling in of the grave. These official orders granted permission for the cemetery to place the casket or remains into the grave, then seal it again. These records usually provide the name, gender, age, date and location of death, cause of death, burial place, and cemetery plot number, plus the undertaker's name.

DEATH CERTIFICATES

Death certificates may also be included in cemetery papers, depending on how detailed the superintendent was at the time. We'll talk about death certificates in more detail in chapter 9, but for now we just want to note they may help us pinpoint an epidemic that ravaged the community at the time.

In image **K**, we see that Charles A. Plummer died on August 28, 1881. He was a white thirteen-year-old boy who was born in Indiana and lived in Evansville, Indiana, his entire life. Both of his parents came from New York State. Near the bottom of the form, we see that

Charles died of typhoid fever, a bacterial disease that is contagious. It begins with an eruption of red spots on the chest and abdomen followed by a high fever, usually around 104 degrees, with abdominal pain, constipation, and headaches. By the third week, the infected person is emaciated and suffering from delusions and mental disturbances. If

☞ The Special Attention of Physicians is respectfully invited to the NAMES BELOW, and to the
List of Diseases on the BACK OF THIS CERTIFICATE.

The Board of Health of the City of Evansville
HAS MADE THE FOLLOWING ORDER :

" No Burial can be made without a proper Certificate. The Physician who attended any person in a last illness is responsible for the preparation of this Certificate, accurately filled out, within thirty-six hours after said person's death."

Certificate of Death.

1. Full Name of Deceased | Write legibly and spell correctly. If an infant not named, give parents' names. | *Charles A Plummer*

2. Date of Death *August 28" 1881*

3. Age, *13* years, *7* months, *18* days. Color, *White*

4. Single, ~~Married, Widow or Widower~~, | Cross out the words not required in this line. | 5. Occupation

6. Birthplace | State or Country | *Ind* | How long in the United States, if of foreign birth |

7. How long a resident in this city *During entire life*

8. Father's Birthplace, | State or Country | *N.B.*

9. Mother's Birthplace, | State or Country | *N.B.*

10. Place of Death, No. *1108 E Ill* Street, *6* Ward.

11. Cause of Death was *Typhoid fever*

12. Length of time Sick *Four weeks*

Signed by

W.S. Pollard *M.D.*

MEDICAL ATTENDANT.

Image K: Looking at death certificates for several people in a town can clue you into any major epidemics that may have affected the area.

untreated, ten to thirty percent of those infected died of the disease, which was spread by eating or drinking food or water contaminated by the feces of an infected person. As the death certificate shows, Charles lasted four weeks after he contracted the disease.

From this death certificate, we can start an investigation to see if a rash of typhoid deaths were sweeping through Evansville, Indiana, during that period of time. Another Evansville-born preteen, fourteen-year-old Alleen Compton, contracted typhoid around the same time as Charles and died three days after Charles did. That information can lead us to search for other family members of these two boys to find out if others succumbed as well.

GRAVESTONE INSCRIPTIONS

Many graves are marked with only the deceased's name and death date, and some also include birth and marriage dates. But more detailed gravestone inscriptions can tell us a lot about the deceased: their lives, their families and their roles in them, their marital and economic statuses, their religions, their occupations, and information about any military service and any organizations and clubs they belonged to.

Inscriptions, or epitaphs, are short pieces of text or symbols inscribed on a tombstone that honor a deceased person, provide information about her, or act as a message (perhaps a warning) to the living. How someone is remembered can tell us a lot about who he was, his status in his family and community, and the period of time in which he lived. Many times the deceased selected her own epitaph. If not, a loved one or family member might do so.

As a result, epitaphs are as distinctive and varied as the people they honor. Many times epitaphs are heartfelt, informative, and enduring, while others are short and to the point. An epitaph can be descriptive, religious, thought-provoking, humorous, or an expression of grief or love. Some even contain poems, Bible verses, or inspirational quotes, giving some insight into the deceased's values (image **L**). It all depends on the personality of the person who was buried there.

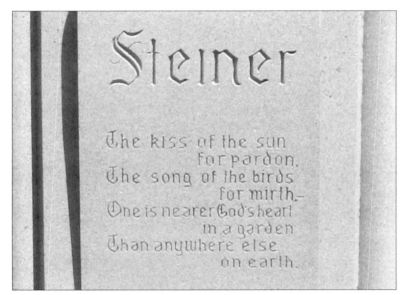

Image L: Some graves have more literary inscriptions, such as this one bearing the "Kiss of the Sun" poem.

But in addition to giving us clues about the deceased's personality and values, epitaphs can indicate other key aspects of a person's life. We'll spend the rest of the chapter discussing how epitaphs can suggest different characteristics of a person's life.

Relationships

Relationships, even if only indicated by a single word (image **M**), can tell us who this person was and indicate further records to search: wife (the person was married), mother/father (the person had children), sister/brother (the person had siblings). Relationships also help us establish more ancestors in this line.

Marital Status

Wife and husband are easy enough to understand, but there are other marital terms you may not recognize that can be found on older stones. One such term is "consort," which is used to describe the (non-ruling) spouse of a monarch—for example, Queen Elizabeth II's consort is

Image M: Titles and family relationships on tombstones can give you clues about what to research next.

Image N: "Consort" on a tombstone indicates that the deceased died before his spouse.

Image O: People were sometimes buried with multiple spouses and family members.

Breathing Life into Tombstones:
Nathaniel Willis, Father of the Year

Nathaniel Parker Willis from Crawfordsville, Indiana, was murdered, and his monument tells his story. Nathaniel, born in 1868, apprenticed for the local newspaper before setting out as a salesman. His first wife died young, so he married Hattie Bell of Ladoga, Indiana, and had a daughter, Mary Frances Laura Willis.

Reports indicate the marriage was not a happy one. In fact, Hattie took Mary and ran away shortly after they relocated to Indianapolis for Nathaniel's new sales position. Nathaniel searched throughout Indiana for his daughter until he learned she had been taken down south to Little Rock, Arkansas, with Hattie and her new "husband," W.Y. Ellis.

Nathaniel longed to see his daughter again. He knew appealing to Hattie's sense of fairness would do no good, so he followed her to Arkansas. Nathaniel made an appointment to appear before the court in Little Rock to receive permission for his daughter to visit him at his hotel. On the morning of July 27, 1909, Nathaniel arrived at the courthouse, climbing the steps with high hopes of spending time with Mary: perhaps taking a stroll down Main Street or sharing a fresh glass of buttermilk. Nathaniel entered the muggy courtroom and sat down, fanning himself with his hat as he waited his turn before the bench. Behind him, the door opened. All eyes turned to the back of the room, and Nathaniel sensed something amiss. As he glanced behind, a shot rang out. Nathaniel slumped to the floor, shot dead by W.Y. Ellis.

During Ellis's murder trial, prosecutors showed that Nathaniel had followed all legal manners necessary to secure his rights to visit with his daughter, having devoted his life to finding her. His friends were outraged by the incident. Although Ellis was found guilty, Nathaniel's friends felt helpless that nothing more could be done.

That's when the Crawfordsville townsfolk had an idea. Working together, they built a monument to Nathaniel and Mary, explaining what happened on that hot summer day.

Today that monument stands in Oak Hill Cemetery, marking the grave of Nathaniel Willis and telling the story of his fatherly love and devotion for Mary.

Prince Phillip. But when the word is found on a woman's gravestone in the United States, it indicates that she was married and died before her husband. Similarly, the term is found on a man's stone when he was married and passed away before his wife (image **N**).

In a similar vein, the term "relict" describes a woman who was a widow at the time of her death. It may also indicate a widower, but it's seldom seen on men's graves of the late eighteenth and early nineteenth centuries—possibly because men remarried more often than women.

When you're in the cemetery, always check the names on the graves near family members to see if there might be another spouse buried nearby (image **O**). Many times the husband will be buried between two wives, so check the dates and do some sleuthing to find out more.

Religion

A word or emblem carved on the stone or erected near the grave can indicate what faith your ancestor professed to. Crucifixes generally indicate Roman Catholicism (image **P**), for example, while plain crosses could refer to a wider variety of religious denominations.

Keep in mind that cemeteries run by religious organizations were not always exclusive to adherents of that faith. For example, Grandma Matilda may be buried in a Baptist church's cemetery, but that does not mean she really converted from Catholicism. In that case, you should check with both religious institutions when searching for her records.

Occupation and Economic Status

A job can be a status symbol, and many people were very proud of what they did for a living. Some were so proud they had it carved on their tombstones for the world to see, sometimes even including the company's name (image **Q**). Others indicated their occupations with a symbol: a train carved on the stone of a railroad engineer (image **R**), or a cask for the local barrel maker.

The size and shape of the stone/monument can also indicate the social status or economic position your ancestor held. A small concrete slab with painted letters tells a different story than a marble mausoleum, or a monument with the bust of the deceased carved on the front.

Image P: Religious imagery on graves, such as a crucifix, can direct you to church records.

Image Q: Some workers were so proud of the company they worked for that they mentioned it on their graves.

Image R: Andrew Erwin was a railroad engineer, and proud of it.

Setting Goals

To get maximum results from your research, set some defined goals. Take time to decide what ancestor(s) you are looking for, what records and information you want to find, and where you will be searching. Are you searching to discover what family members are buried here, or are you looking for someone specific? Is this trip just to research burial records and talk with the sexton? Or, are you hoping to walk the cemetery and visit the graves? Once you've set tangible goals, you can take the necessary steps and visit the places that may have the answers, and records, you seek.

As a former journalist, I always approach my cemetery research with a nod to the Five W's: who, what, when, where, and why. Who are you searching for? What are your goals for this trip? When is the time period you will be investigating? Where are you planning to go, and what other groups will you be contacting for backup or assistance? And why are you searching for this information? (To add to your family tree? To join a group like the Daughters of the American Revolution? For possible health-related information?) Once you've determined why you're going to a cemetery, what you want to accomplish, and how to achieve it, you're ready to begin the actual groundwork at the cemetery, what I consider the fun part of the investigation.

Military

We are a nation proud of its military men and women, so military service is usually designated on a gravestone in some form. If the person died in a battle, the marker may list the unit he served in, rank held, and the war (image **S**). An emblem or plaque may also be located in front or on the back of the stone with more service details (image **T**).

Symbols

We have used symbols for thousands of years to convey our thoughts, feelings, and desires. Gravestones became more ornate in the mid-1800s

Image S: Military graves are often marked by the symbol of the branch the deceased served in, or with a marker indicating the conflict(s) he served in.

Image T: Some gravestones provide more specific information about the deceased's military service.

during the Victorian era, and these carvings held special meanings and offer insight into a person's life. This "silent language" was a way to honor a loved one and provide comfort to those left behind.

Several symbols can adorn a single stone, and the layers of meanings can tell the story, offering a glimpse into the deceased's life and interests. Other symbols may be secret messages with the meanings known only to the family, the deceased, or the stonecarver. We'll look at tombstone inscriptions and symbols in more detail in chapters 5 and 6.

KEYS from the CRYPT

• Seek out a variety of records at a cemetery (such as cemetery deeds, sexton's records, and burial transit permits), not just tombstone inscriptions.

• Read and take note of everything that appears on a gravestone, as each symbol, word, and date has meaning. We'll discuss tombstone inscriptions in more detail in chapters 5 and 6.

• Set defined goals for your trip to the cemetery. Outline who you're searching for, the time period, who you will contact while you're there, and why you are searching for this information.

Cemetery Records Checklist

Tombstones are crucial subjects of study during any trip to the cemetery, but they're not the only records you should seek while on hallowed ground. Use this checklist to make sure you've fully researched your ancestors:

Ancestor's name _____

Cemetery name _____

Burial records
- ☐ Burial permits
- ☐ Burial transit permits
- ☐ Grave opening permits
- ☐ Grave closing permits

Gravestone records
- ☐ Tombstone inscriptions
- ☐ Cemetery deeds
- ☐ Plot records
- ☐ Plat maps

Other records
- ☐ Sexton's records
- ☐ Cemetery ledger
- ☐ Death certificates

Finding Your Ancestors' Graves

Image A: Visiting an ancestor's grave, as I did to my great-grandmother's, can be powerful.

There is something magical about standing at an ancestor's grave (image **A**). There we suddenly *feel* the pull of all those generations, realizing that this person was a part our family and a part of our DNA. And that is when those questions begin: What did she believe? What did he do for a living? What were their lives like back then? Suddenly we find ourselves seeking answers. Before we know it, genealogy has reeled us in, and we *have* to know more about these ancestors we've felt a new connection to.

As a result, finding your ancestor's tombstone is an important step on your journey to researching your family's history. And like other kinds of genealogy research, cemetery research is increasingly accessible online, with large databases dedicated to archiving grave locations and digitizing tombstone and burial records.

In this chapter, we'll outline two of the major tools available to tombstone tourists and genealogists—BillionGraves and Find A Grave—along with information on how to use them.

BILLIONGRAVES

BillionGraves <www.billiongraves.com> is the world's largest free directory of searchable GPS cemetery information, and the site strives to record, preserve, and make available worldwide at least one billion grave photos with GPS coordinates. With more than 17 million GPS headstone records to date, BillionGraves is well on its way to accomplishing that goal, and it's developed record-sharing partnerships with FamilySearch <www.familysearch.org> and MyHeritage <www.myheritage.com>.

Getting Started

You can begin searching for an ancestor on the BillionGraves homepage (image **B**). While BillionGraves is free to use (and you can search for your ancestors' graves as an unregistered user), creating an account on the site will allow you to add and edit record entries and communicate with other users. To register, go to the homepage and click the Login with Facebook or Log-In button at the top of the page, then select Continue as [Your Name] to connect your Facebook account or Register (for

Image B: BillionGraves is one of the web's largest databases of headstones and their locations.

e-mail). If you're not signing in through Facebook, you'll need to enter an e-mail address and password.

From the main toolbar, you can access BillionGraves' best features under Research. Here you can access the search form (Search Records) and connect your BillionGraves information to online family trees (BillionGraves Tree). The Research tab also hosts the Cemetery Map, which shows hundreds of cemeteries located in your region. Once you have an account, you can store gravestone photos (Add Photos/My Photo Map) and gravestones you've saved (Favorite Graves). The BG Photo Requests function <**www.billiongraves.com/cemetery-requests**>, accessible under My Photo Requests and Nearby Requests, is an especially useful feature. Here, you can upload a request for a specific grave that you'd like another researcher to photograph and add to the BillionGraves database or—if you're feeling charitable—where you can fulfill another's request. The Nearby Requests page will even let you view what requests are near your current location. Click one of the gravestone pins on a map to view the request, then hit Accept Request to take it on.

The Get Help tab is a great resource, too, with how-to videos, blog posts, and assistance from the BillionGraves community. This is the perfect place to ask a question, research answers, or request support.

Whether or not you created an account on BillionGraves, you can search for your ancestors either from the homepage <**www.billiongraves. com**> (under Find Their Graves) or from the main search form <**www. billiongraves.com/search**> (also accessible by clicking the blue Search BillionGraves button on the site's main toolbar). Here's what to do next:

STEP 1 Enter your search terms. From the main page, simply enter the first and last names of the ancestor whose grave you're searching for. If you're searching from the main search page, you'll see additional options: birth and death years (with a dropdown box allowing you to select a range of years), country, state, and county. The search form even allows you to filter your results by Exact Match (results that exactly match your search terms), Phonetic (results that sound similar to your search terms), or Record Type (headstone, death certificate, etc.). You can also search by cemetery by clicking the Cemeteries tab, which allows you to search by cemetery name, country, state, and county. Once you've entered your search terms, click Search.

1

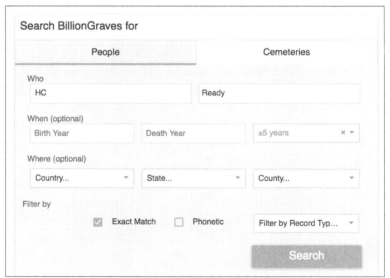

STEP 2 Review your results. The site will retrieve records that match your terms. Each result lists the name on/in the record, an image that describes what kind of record it is, the years associated with the record, and the name and place of the cemetery it appears in. Note that you may need to refine your search results; you can do so by changing any of the fields in the left column under Refine Results and clicking Refine Search. For example, when I searched for *HC Ready*, the results returned no matches, but revising the search with a space between the H and C resulted in several options.

STEP 3 See record details. When you click on a result, you'll be taken to a page detailing the record, beginning with "Life Information," a summary of the deceased's known biography. Registered users can edit record details or add additional information to the record by clicking the plus sign (to add) or the pencil (to edit). The dots allow you to connect this record to a person on FamilySearch's Family Tree or report a problem. In this example, H.C. Ready was a Civil War soldier who died on September 7, 1863.

STEP 4 View the cemetery. The info under Grave Site provides any records of other people named Ready who are buried in the cemetery, plus the cemetery's name, address, and website. You can also view an interactive map of the cemetery's location; toggle between a street map and satellite map by clicking the appropriate tabs in the top-left corner, and zoom in and out using the plus and minus signs in the bottom right. H.C.'s record shows that the cemetery is on Rozier Street and provides us with the name and address of the burial ground: the Confederate Cemetery in Alton, Illinois.

GRAVE TIP

Try, Try, Try Again: If you've searched for several family names on BillionGraves or Find A Grave but still get no results, don't worry. Remember: These sites are works in progress. What you didn't find last month might be listed this month. Of course, you can always upload the graves near you to get your family entered into the database.

2

Search Results

H C Ready
Birth Year: Not Available
Death Year: 1863

Confederate Cemetery
Alton, Illinois, United States

H. C. Ready
Birth Year: Not Available
Death Year: 1863

Alton Cemetery
Alton, Illinois, United States

We found records about H C READY

3

Life Information

Record taken from the U.S. Department of Veterans Affairs for H C Ready.

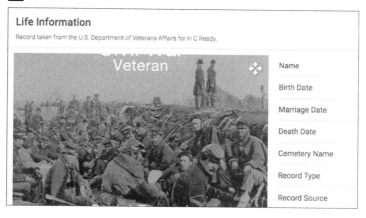

Name

Birth Date

Marriage Date

Death Date

Cemetery Name

Record Type

Record Source

4

Grave Site

H C Ready is buried in the Confederate Cemetery at the location displayed on the map below. This GPS information is ONLY available at BillionGraves. Our technolog...
gravesite and other family members buried nearby.

Nearby Family

Nearby Records	0
READY Family in Confederate Cemetery	1

Cemetery Information

Cemetery Name	Confederate Cemetery
Cemetery Website	http://www.cem.va.gov/cems/lo...
Cemetery Address	706-948 Rozier St Alton, Madison, Illinois United States

STEP 5 Explore other records on MyHeritage. The MyHeritage section will direct you to other records that might be connected to H.C. Ready's life, including birth, marriage, death, and census records. Note that you'll need a MyHeritage subscription to access that site's records.

STEP 6 Evaluate family information. The Family tab allows you to view relationships indicated on the headstone as well as those added by other users. Registered users can also add relationship information as it appears on the headstone—simply click the plus

5

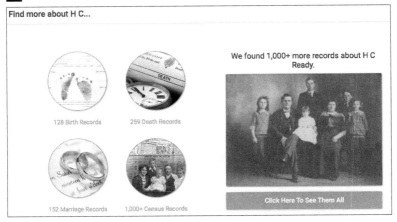

Find more about H C...

128 Birth Records   259 Death Records

152 Marriage Records   1,000+ Census Records

We found 1,000+ more records about H C Ready.

Click Here To See Them All

6

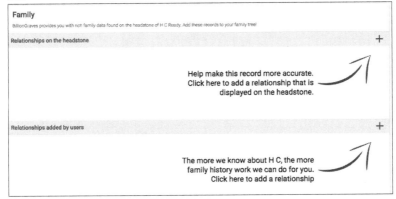

Family

BillionGraves provides you with rich family data found on the headstone of H C Ready. Add these records to your family tree!

Relationships on the headstone   +

Help make this record more accurate. Click here to add a relationship that is displayed on the headstone.

Relationships added by users   +

The more we know about H C, the more family history work we can do for you. Click here to add a relationship

Digging into Cemeteries on BillionGraves

The digitized records on BillionGraves may contain vital information about your ancestors, but they're only half the story. BillionGraves also has profiles on individual cemeteries that can reveal valuable information about your ancestors and the times they lived in. To view information about a cemetery, click the cemetery's name under the Grave Site tab on the records page, or find a cemetery using the Cemeteries tab on the main search page.

On a cemetery's page, you can read more about it, including a brief history, its operating hours, directions, photos, and even a map of where records appear in the cemetery. This gives you a fascinating historical brief that can provide research leads and colorful depictions of your ancestor's life and times.

For example, the description for the North Alton Confederate Cemetery is a harrowing tale: The prison was abandoned by the state due to the "unhealthy conditions," but nearly two thousand prisoners (more than twice the maximum capacity) were held there during the war. Disease—especially smallpox—ran rampant, and those who died in the prison were buried on Tow Head Island, only to have their remains washed away when the Mississippi River flooded over the years. In 1909, the United Daughters of the Confederacy erected a monument for the 1,354 prisoners who died on Tow Head Island—including H.C. Ready. The page even has a photo of the granite memorial obelisk.

In addition, you can view a list of other geographically close burial sites under Nearby Cemeteries. For example, eight graveyards reside in a 2.5-mile radius of the North Alton Confederate Cemetery, only two of which have BillionGrave images associated with them.

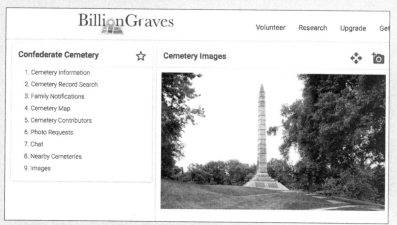

You can also learn about individual cemeteries on BillionGraves.

7

Other Sources   +

BillionGraves has teamed up with partners to provide CONFIRMED matches to other sources. Find more family by viewing other records for H C Ready.

Click here to add a supporting record ⟍

sign and enter the information, then hit Add Relationship. If you want to add other relationships (i.e., those that aren't mentioned on the headstone), click the plus sign under Relationships added by users, then search for a record of the appropriate person.

STEP 7 Add other sources. Registered users can also add connections between BillionGraves records or upload new records about the deceased. First, click the plus sign under the Other Sources tab, then select from the options of records (Burial Record, Death Certificate, Headstone Image, Historic Record, Memorial Plaque/Monument, Obituary, or Other). Follow the prompts to add the source to the burial entry. (Note: You'll have the option of adding an image of the source. Click Skip under the drag-and-drop box if you don't have one.)

STEP 8 Read and share memories. The Memories tab allows you to write, in your own words, what you remember, or have learned about your ancestor. Simply click the plus sign to get started. You'll simply title the memory, then write and format your memory in the window that pops up. Make sure you click Save when you're finished!

STEP 9 View your ancestor's military service information. If the deceased served in the military, you can view his rank, branch, and conflict—and registered users can add or edit this information.

Using the Mobile App

So far, we've discussed how to use BillionGraves on a desktop computer or laptop, but the site also has a powerful mobile app that can revolutionize your cemetery research while you're in the field. Download the BillionGraves app (available for free on both iOS and Android) to view a cemetery record while you're on the ground in the cemetery. With a dynamic GPS map, the app will allow you to search archived headstone images near your location. Here's how:

8

Add a Memory

H.C. Ready

File ▾   Edit ▾   Insert ▾   View ▾   Format ▾

B *I* U ▤ ▤ ↰ ↱ ▣ 𝒫 ⁑

H.C. Ready was a soldier in the Confederate Army during the Civil War.

9

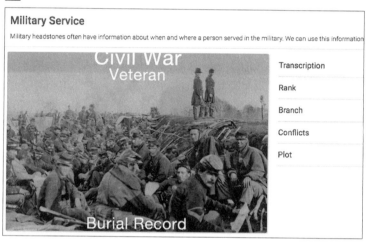

Military Service

Military headstones often have information about when and where a person served in the military. We can use this information

Civil War
Veteran

Transcription	
Rank	
Branch	
Conflicts	
Plot	

Burial Record

BillionGraves Plus

Upgrading to the premium BillionGraves Plus subscription removes ads and gives you priority tech support. Plus subscribers also receive four services that non-paying users do not:

- Nearby Graves: Allows you to virtually visit cemeteries anywhere in the world by "walking" the rows of headstones searching for other graves with your family's name
- Family Plots: Uses GPS technology to locate where your ancestors are buried all over the world
- Family Notifications: Updates you when an ancestor's grave is added
- Global Family GPS mapping: Zooms in on cities, states, countries, even large regions of the world to show where your ancestors traveled—and where those elusive burial grounds might be

STEP 1 Download the BillionGraves Camera App onto your smartphone. The app is free, and is available for both iOS and Android.

STEP 2 Sign into your account (if you have one). Click Dashboard to log in to your account or—if you're not already a BillionGraves user—to register a new account. This will allow you to access your saved graves and upload pictures from the field; see chapter 8 for more on the latter.

STEP 3 Search for a person's name. Tap the Records button, then enter your search information; tap Advanced to go to a search form with more options. This will conduct a similar search to the one you can perform on the desktop site. If you're not looking for a particular ancestor and you just want to see what graves are nearest to you, click Show Nearest on the search form. You can also view graves you've saved by clicking Favorites.

STEP 4 View your results. Tap on the person's name to bring up an image of the gravestone and its transcription, plus the headstone's location on a zoomable map (click the map icon in the bottom right corner).

While in the field, you'll also likely want to upload photos and grave locations to BillionGraves; see chapter 8 for details on how to do this.

FIND A GRAVE

Find A Grave <www.findagrave.com> is an online database of cemetery records from around the world. Owned by Ancestry.com <www.ancestry.com>, Find A Grave offers 159 million grave records and 75 million photos submitted by more than four hundred thousand registered contributors. In addition to allowing you to search all these records and images, the site

GRAVE TIP

Search Local Societies: If a village or township cemetery doesn't have its own website, check the local genealogical or historical societies for maps or contact information. These local organizations sometimes step in to provide the services (or expertise) that the cemeteries lack.

1

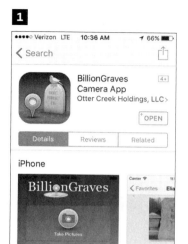

2

3

4

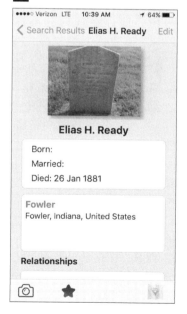

allows you to create virtual memorials that can contain virtual flowers, biographies, photos, and other pertinent information. Find A Grave also has a section where you can search for famous graves, view interesting monuments and epitaphs, or browse by the "claim to fame" search tool. The site also allows you to request volunteers in the area to do a lookup and post their findings on the site.

Getting Started with Find A Grave

While Find A Grave is totally free to use, you'll want to create an account to be able to add and edit entries, photos, memories, and more. You can register by clicking the Join now! link next to the website's name on the homepage. You'll be asked for an e-mail address and password, plus your name and a "Public Name" that you'd like to be known as on the site. You can also add your ZIP code and sign up to be a photo volunteer who fulfills photo requests in an area. Once you register, you'll receive an e-mail with a registration code that you'll need to enter to access your account.

Find A Grave entries are called "memorials," and they're created to help remember the deceased. Memorials can include vital information (including burial/death dates and places), as well as memories, virtual flowers left by mourners, photos, and relationships to other people.

Searching for and Viewing Records

STEP 1 **Enter your search terms.** Go to Find A Grave's homepage <www.findagrave.com> and select Search 162 million grave records under the Find Graves heading or (if you're elsewhere on the site) click Begin New Search from the left column under Actions. In addition to first, middle, and last names, you can also include birth and death years (with before/in/after modifiers), the cemetery's location, and (if you've already found the entry on Find A Grave) memorial number. In this search, I looked for my maternal grandfather, Robert Dellinger (1908–2000).

STEP 2 **Review your results.** The search returns memorials that match your criteria. Each result will list the name on the memorial, plus associated birth and death dates and the name and location of the cemetery. Icons (see the Icon Key, at right) indicate what other information is mentioned. My search returned just one result, and it seems like the right one. A flower indicates someone has left virtual flowers at the memorial, and the Mona Lisa head and headstone icons indicate the memorial contains a photo of the deceased and an image of his headstone, respectively.

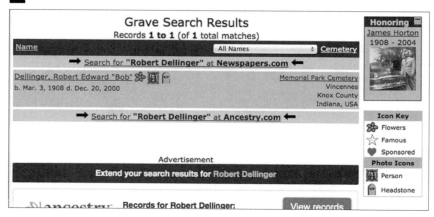

1

Find A Grave Search Form

Name: Robert | E | Dellinger
First | Middle | Last (required)

Include maiden name(s) in my search ☐
Do partial name search on surname ☐

Born: In | **Year:** 1908
Died: In | **Year:** 2000
Cemetery in: The United States
– US State List –
Memorial #:
Date filter: All Names
Order by: Name

Search

2

Grave Search Results
Records **1 to 1** (of **1** total matches)

Honoring
James Horton
1908 - 2004

| Name | All Names | Cemetery |

➡ Search for **"Robert Dellinger"** at **Newspapers.com** ⬅

Dellinger, Robert Edward "Bob" 🌸 🖼 | Memorial Park Cemetery
b. Mar. 3, 1908 d. Dec. 20, 2000 | Vincennes
Knox County
Indiana, USA

➡ Search for **"Robert Dellinger"** at **Ancestry.com** ⬅

Icon Key
🌸 Flowers
☆ Famous
♥ Sponsored
Photo Icons
🖼 Person
🪦 Headstone

Advertisement
Extend your search results for Robert Dellinger

Ancestry **Records for Robert Dellinger:** View records

STEP 3 View the memorial. Click the person's name to be transported to his or her memorial page. You'll see a wide variety of information based on who has added to the memorial and how much has been contributed. My grandfather's page contains his birth and death dates and places, plus a written summary of his life, photos of him and his tombstone, and his wife's name and vital information (with a link to her memorial page).

STEP 4 Learn more about the cemetery. Click the name of a cemetery to go to its page on Find A Grave, which contains a brief history of the cemetery, a summary of its records (including how many famous interments it holds), a list of photo requests from the cemetery, and the cemetery's phone number and website address. You can even search the cemetery from this page. Click the Map tab to view an interactive map of the cemetery and its surrounding community.

Death Styles of the Rich and Famous

Although it's been over twenty years since Find A Grave began, the site has always stayed close to its roots. You can still search for graves of well-known people by date, including those born on or died on a certain date, or by using the "Claim to Fame" feature. Interesting monuments and epitaphs, posthumous reunions, and yearly necrologies provide interesting perusing.

Find Famous Graves

See the graves of thousands of famous people from around the world.

- Famous Grave Search
- Browse by **Location**
- Browse by **Claim to Fame**
- Search by **Date**
  -Born On This Date
  -Died On This Date
- **Most Popular** Searches
- Yearly Necrologies
- Posthumous Reunions
- Interesting Monuments
- Interesting Epitaphs
- New Listings
- New Photos

Find A Grave has a large database of celebrities' gravesites.

3

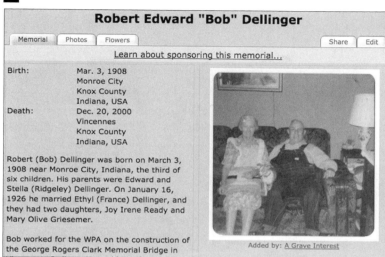

Robert Edward "Bob" Dellinger

| Memorial | Photos | Flowers | | Share | Edit |

Learn about sponsoring this memorial...

Birth: Mar. 3, 1908
Monroe City
Knox County
Indiana, USA

Death: Dec. 20, 2000
Vincennes
Knox County
Indiana, USA

Robert (Bob) Dellinger was born on March 3, 1908 near Monroe City, Indiana, the third of six children. His parents were Edward and Stella (Ridgeley) Dellinger. On January 16, 1926 he married Ethyl (France) Dellinger, and they had two daughters, Joy Irene Ready and Mary Olive Griesemer.

Bob worked for the WPA on the construction of the George Rogers Clark Memorial Bridge in

Added by: A Grave Interest

4

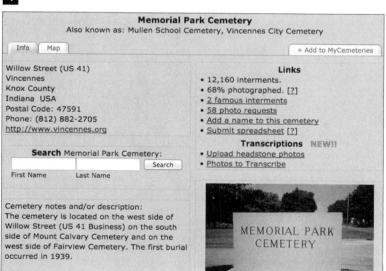

Memorial Park Cemetery
Also known as: Mullen School Cemetery, Vincennes City Cemetery

| Info | Map | | + Add to MyCemeteries |

Willow Street (US 41)
Vincennes
Knox County
Indiana USA
Postal Code: 47591
Phone: (812) 882-2705
http://www.vincennes.org

Links
- 12,160 interments.
- 68% photographed. [?]
- 2 famous interments
- 58 photo requests
- Add a name to this cemetery
- Submit spreadsheet [?]

Transcriptions NEW!!
- Upload headstone photos
- Photos to Transcribe

Search Memorial Park Cemetery:

| | | Search |
First Name   Last Name

Cemetery notes and/or description:
The cemetery is located on the west side of Willow Street (US 41 Business) on the south side of Mount Calvary Cemetery and on the west side of Fairview Cemetery. The first burial occurred in 1939.

MEMORIAL PARK
CEMETERY

Like BillionGraves, Find A Grave also has a mobile app for iOS and Android devices that allows you to take the site's resources into the field.

STEP 1 Download the free Find A Grave app. Once you download and open the app, read the instructional information. You'll then be directed to a screen that gives you three options: Search for a Memorial, Search for a Cemetery, and My Profile.

STEP 2 Log in to your account. Click My Profile to log in to your existing Find A Grave account or to create a new account. This will allow you to save search results and upload photos.

STEP 3 Start your search. Click Search for a Memorial to look for individual records. Each mirrors the respective search pages on the desktop website. On the Memorial Search page, enter your ancestor's name (note the Last Name field is listed first on the form) and birth/death information, plus a cemetery location. Click Search in the top right to submit your query.

STEP 4 View your results. Click a search result to view the memorial's page. In addition to images of the person or grave and any associated

2

3

4

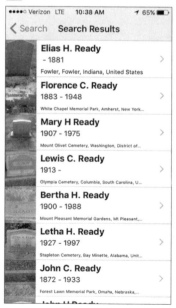

birth/death dates, you can also view the address of the cemetery the tombstone resides in, sometimes with plot information. Click More to add or update the grave's GPS coordinates, share with others via various apps, save to your personal graves, or (if you're logged in and listed as the memorial's manager) edit or delete the memorial; see chapter 8 for more on these options. You can also request a photo of this grave by clicking Request in the top left, next to the camera icon.

You can also search for cemeteries by clicking Search for a Cemetery from the main page, or by clicking Cemetery Search from the menu (click the three bars at the top of the left column from most screens within the app). The app will show cemeteries near your geographic location by default, but you can search more distant cemeteries by using the search bar at top. Tap a cemetery on the map to view its page, where you can view memorials that were created from headstones in the cemetery, add headstone photos or memorials, and view the cemetery's address and contact info.

LOCAL CEMETERY SITES

Massive databases such as BillionGraves and Find A Grave aren't the only online resources that tombstone researchers should utilize. Many individual cemeteries have useful websites that can provide a wealth of information, including photos and maps of the grounds, a brief history of the cemetery, and what records are available to genealogists.

Generally, the smaller the cemetery (and the smaller the workforce), the less information you'll find online. That being said, always check for a website—regardless of the cemetery's size—because many cemeteries will have at least some information (such as its operating hours and address) online. Many municipal cemeteries, for example, have only a web page that's part of the city or town's government website, but from it you can get the name of the superintendent, office hours, and a phone number. Some small cemeteries also have dedicated groups of volunteers who create great websites with plenty of photos, guides and maps, and local histories. Others even offer GPS smartphone tours of the grounds.

Some cemetery websites even have sections geared toward genealogists and historians, often labeled as "Genealogists," "Our History," or "About Us." Here, you might find a detailed history of the grounds, along with information on notable/famous people buried there and details on elaborate monuments, sculptures, and architecture. Keep an eye out for links to local, regional, and state websites that can help with your research, plus any connections to local genealogical or historical societies.

If you're lucky, the cemetery that holds your ancestor's grave will have a search function to help you find burial records. Some cemeteries have digitized their collections of burial records (or at least provided indexes for them), while others will require you to request look-ups, possibly for a fee. To perform a search, you'll generally need at least a surname and death date (plus, obviously, the name of the cemetery).

Let's take a look at three great local cemetery websites to see what researchers can look for.

The Big and Beautiful: Bellefontaine Cemetery (St. Louis, MO)

Bellefontaine Cemetery is home to many of the elite movers and shakers of St. Louis. Built as a rural cemetery, it became popular during the mid-1800s. These highly landscaped "Cities of the Dead" featured walking paths, abundant landscaping and shady trees, decorative monuments, fresh air and water, statues, gorgeous architecture, and a chance for folks to stroll the cemetery grounds and escape the dirt and grime of the eighth largest city in the United States for a few restful hours.

In addition to being a beautiful place to spend an afternoon, Bellefontaine has one of the most professional-looking cemetery websites I've found <bellefontainecemetery.org> (image **C**). With plenty of style, this site features numerous tools that a family researcher will find useful, plus photos, maps, tons of historical information, burial search options, and the choice of exploring the grounds or planning a funeral.

While I don't have family buried in Bellefontaine, I wish I did—this website makes it easy to search for your ancestor and learn a bit about him. Start with the "Burial Search" button (image **D**), where you can search for burial records on an interactive map of the cemetery and create a printable report that you can bring with you into the field. Or you can click "Visits and Tours" on the main page to access "Tips for Visiting," which lists hours of operation, directions, and etiquette for visitors. Here you can also view an interactive map of the grounds (image **E**) that allows you to tour the cemetery based on your interests: "architecture, movers and shakers, scalawags or champion trees." A downloadable mobile app (available through the Apple App Store or via Google Play) allows you to take a self-guided journey through the grounds. Also check out the "Historical Stories" link to see if there is any information about your ancestor.

The website has other attractions that might interest you. Under the "Destination" tab, explore the cemetery's horticulture, history, art and architecture, and wildlife. Just hover the arrow over any tab and a small snippet of information will inform you what to expect. Teachers can also check out the "Education" link at the top of the page, which provides information about the official cemetery book.

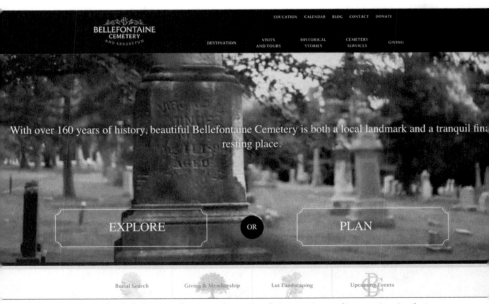

Image C: The Bellefontaine Cemetery has a visually interesting and interactive site that lets you learn more about your ancestors.

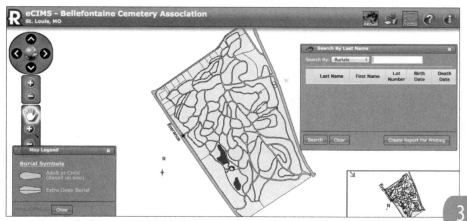

Image D: Some cemetery websites, like Bellefontaine Cemetery's, have robust search tools. This search page will even plot search results on a map.

Image E: This interactive map allows you to view different kinds of attractions on a map of the cemetery.

Crown Hill Cemetery is the third largest non-government cemetery in the country. The cemetery was created by the US government in 1863 as a national cemetery for Union soldiers when Union Civil War dead filled up another local cemetery. Over the years, the cemetery became more beautiful (adding a limestone Gothic chapel that holds nearly one hundred crypts) and more inclusive, adding the Confederate Mound, a final resting place for 1,616 Confederate soldiers, in 1933. The last veteran, Vietnam War pilot Major Robert W. Hayes, was buried in the cemetery in 1969.

The Crown Hill website <**www.crownhill.org**> (image **F**) is easy to use and provides everything a family researcher wants to know. Under the Cemetery tab, simply click "Locate a Loved One" to locate the "Burial Locater" form (image **G**), where you can enter the first and last names of your ancestor along with his birth year. The dropdown menu

Image F: Crown Hill, which operates both a cemetery and a funeral home, offers several features on its website, including resources for family historians.

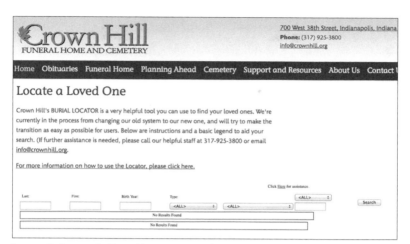

Image G: You can find burial locations using the "Locate a Loved One" page on Crown Hill Cemetery's website.

for "Type" offers several selections for burial options, including ground space, lawn crypt, and mausoleum. The last box allows you to enter any other info you might know.

The Cemetery Tab has a few other goodies for researchers. The History section provides a timeline where you can see what was happening when your family lived in Indianapolis and when your ancestor was buried in the cemetery. The Notable Persons tab offers a list of the more famous people who are buried here. For instance Lyman S. Ayres (founder of L.S. Ayres Department stores) is interred here, along with Dr. Richard Gatling (inventor of the Gatling gun) and famed 1930s gangster John Dillinger.

Public tours of the cemetery are held from June through October, and you can also arrange private tours. Several tours are themed, which can add a certain drama to visiting the cemetery if the era described is also that of your ancestor. A Crown Hill book produced by the cemetery might prove valuable to your collection, and you can print off a handy map that contains the cemetery's hours of operation and some notable sites.

Need more information? Crown Hill has a genealogical information request form that will enlist the cemetery staff's help, showing it wants to make genealogy patrons happy. You can find it on the "Locate a Loved One" page, under Genealogy Requests.

Containing about 175 pastoral acres, Oak Hill Cemetery was founded in 1853 to fill the growing river town's need for more burial space, and its massive grounds are impervious to the surrounding city. With picturesque landscaping, curving paths and drives, and plenty of peaceful vistas (including lakes and numerous trees native to Indiana), you can see why this became Evansville's premier cemetery. Oak Hill Cemetery and its older sister cemetery, Locust Cemetery, are owned by the City of Evansville and Vanderburgh County.

Many cemeteries are owned by cities, towns, or municipalities and so contain information about them on government websites, but locating the cemetery page can be confusing. Since neither the Oak Hill nor Locust cemeteries are mentioned on the main website <www.evansvillegov.org>, it's best to start by checking each dropdown list. The

Image H: Some cemeteries that are run by governments will have web pages that are part of the government's website, so you may have to do some navigating to find the appropriate resources.

cemeteries may be found under the "Government" tab by clicking on Department A-C (for *cemetery*). There you will find "City Cemeteries" and information on both burial grounds (image **H**). Once you click the City Cemetery tab, click Database Search, then Oak Hill Cemetery to be directed to a search form. All you need to begin is a last name.

Although its website **<www.evansvillegov.org/index.aspx?page=2383>** lacks some of the bells and whistles of the larger cemeteries, Oak Hill Cemetery still provides the family researcher with valuable information that can connect you to cemetery staff. According to Oak Hill Cemetery Superintendent Chris Cooke, genealogists should plan their trip and enlist the help of cemetery staff, many of whom are happy to help by providing information or providing look-ups. Cooke also said cemetery staff will need last name, first name, age, year (or timeframe) of death, and any surname variations.

Under the "Oak Hill Cemetery" tab, you'll also find the cemetery's rules and regulations, a detailed history of the cemetery, and photos of the grounds, plus a map. The cemetery's web page also offers access to its Facebook page, history about the first interment, and even sheet music of the song that was written about the cemetery in 1906. Also check for scheduled events (such as tours or seminars), and take the printable tree guide for a self-guided tour when you're finished with your research.

KEYS from the CRYPT

• Use online databases like Find A Grave and BillionGraves to find your ancestor's grave before trekking into the cemetery, as these can show you what to look for and even (in BillionGraves' case) a geographic location.

• Research the cemeteries your ancestors are buried in, as well as their tombstone and burial records.

• Figure out if the cemetery your ancestor was buried in has its own website. Some local cemetery sites have digitized burial records and even tombstone images that can make your research quicker.

Cemetery Research Kit Checklist

Cemetery research has changed a lot in the past decade. Few of us carry notebooks and file folders anymore since most of our files are now digitized. Today, you can store information on a website or in the cloud for easy access whenever and wherever you want. Even so, you'll need to bring a few physical items with you to the burial grounds. We'll discuss useful tools to have in the cemetery in chapter 4, but here's the cemetery checklist I use before taking off for a day of ancestor sleuthing:

- ☐ Laptop, iPad, or tablet (for notetaking), along with a car charger
- ☐ Cell phone with GPS mapping system and car charger
- ☐ Maps with directions, stored on a mobile device
- ☐ Plat map of the cemetery, stored on a mobile device
- ☐ Digital camera for high-res photos
- ☐ Camera batteries
- ☐ Extra photo storage card
- ☐ Light reflectors (mirror, portable lights, aluminum foil, etc.)
- ☐ Cash to pay for any record copies the cemetery staff makes for you
- ☐ A hardback binder to keep those copies in
- ☐ List of surname variations on a mobile device or index card
- ☐ Soft paintbrush for clearing grass or dirt off stones
- ☐ Clippers (to trim grass from around stones)
- ☐ Spray bottle containing water (to wet stone for better reading ability)
- ☐ Kneeling pad (for working on stones)
- ☐ Dousing rods (for locating unmarked graves)
- ☐ Bottled water and snacks
- ☐ Moist towelettes for quick clean-ups
- ☐ First-aid kit for minor cuts and scrapes
- ☐ Seasonal items like sunscreen and bug spray (summer), or hand warmers and mufflers (winter)
- ☐ Orange vest (if going to a rural or wooded cemetery)
- ☐ Boots or shoes with tread for more stabilized walking

Gravesite Location Worksheet

Name of deceased	Cemetery Information			Find A Grave memorial number	Notes
	Name	Address	Website		

Find A Grave Worksheet

Account info

Username	
Password	

Memorials to watch

Name of deceased	Lifespan	Memorial number	Page manager

3

PART TWO

RESEARCHING ON HALLOWED GROUND

Cemetery Research Strategies

Graveyards offer a wealth of genealogical information. Inscriptions on a tombstone can indicate a whole host of details about a person's life: birth and death dates, surnames, parents' names, children's names, maiden names, and spouses' names. These gravestones may also point us toward religious affiliations, military service, and membership in fraternal organizations. From this information, we may be able to deduce even more about their lives: what jobs they worked, what epidemics swept through the area at the time they lived there, what wars they fought in. Who knew you could glean so much from a trip to the cemetery?

But these finds don't happen automatically—you'll need to prepare for your insightful trip into the cemeteries that hold all these long-lost family secrets. In this chapter, we'll provide you with strategies for working through the cemetery, plus a list of information to collect and tips for safely viewing and recording headstone information. We'll discuss how to read headstones and interpret iconography in chapters 5 and 6, respectively.

CEMETERY BEST PRACTICES

Cemetery research can be exhilarating, but also time-consuming and exhausting. In order to not get overwhelmed, here are ten steps that will assist you in coming away from a day in the cemetery with facts and figures that empower your research.

Set Goals

The best time to decide what you want to accomplish on a cemetery trip is before you set foot on cemetery grounds, as it will be difficult to remain focused once you've begun your journey. Decide what you want to gain from the visit. For example, are you looking into the life of one ancestor, or an entire family? Are you hoping to talk with the cemetery superintendent, or will perusing the files and forms be enough for this trip? By setting some goals, you'll make sure you stay on track, regardless of the fascinating finds and intriguing information you uncover along the way.

Plan Your Trip

Plan your route. Which cemeteries are you visiting, and how do you plan on getting there? If possible, find an online map of the cemetery to learn how it's laid out. Historical county maps may be useful for older cemeteries and pioneer graveyards, particularly if a cemetery's layout has changed over the decades or centuries. Many state websites offer assistance, providing information and maps listed by county. For family cemeteries, check land records and census forms to pinpoint where the family lived; the cemetery will usually be on their property or that of a nearby neighbor. Visit Google Earth **<www.google.com/earth>** to see if the area you want to search has been photographed.

Schedule Appointments

Call or e-mail everyone you want to speak with during your research trip, and set up the appropriate appointments. Make a list of the groups or people who could have information about or files concerning your family's history. Some potential people of interest include the cemetery sexton, the county trustee, courthouse personnel, and genealogical society members. You might also consider visiting the local library, regional archives, historical associations, or any other group with records to search.

Be sure to allow enough time to get to all of the appointments and to visit with the folks who might have the answers to those important research questions you want to ask. Take time to search family history books; dig through records of births, marriages, and deaths; and have a list of questions that you can ask a society member who's willing to chat. Even if your interviewee can't directly answer your question, he may know whom to contact for more stories about your family or the area. Most people will be happy to meet and talk with you, but the courtesy of working with their schedules is always appreciated.

Pack Your Cemetery Bag

A short trip to the cemetery can easily become an all-day event, so plan ahead and have a cemetery bag packed and ready to go for your outing. The bag doesn't have to be fancy (although actual cemetery bags are available online); something sturdy and dependable will do the trick. Depending on the weather and the season, wear layers of clothing so you can adjust as temperatures change.

4

Here are just a few items to put in your cemetery bag:
- Cell phone and car charger
- Digital camera with *lots* of batteries, and perhaps an extra storage card (See the "Cemetery Horror Stories: The Tree of the Dead" sidebar for my own horror story.)
- Soft paintbrush for clearing grass or dirt off stones
- Scissors to trim grass from around stones
- Spray bottle containing water to clear mud from markers or to wet stones for better reading ability
- Kneeling pad for working on stones
- An 8 x 10 mirror in a sturdy frame to reflect light
- Foil and cardboard to create a makeshift light reflector
- Cemetery forms for notes
- Bottled water and snacks
- First-aid kit for minor cuts and scrapes
- Seasonal items: sunscreen and bug spray (spring through fall), or hand warmers and mufflers (fall through spring)
- Boots or shoes with treads for more stabilized walking

Cemetery Horror Stories: The Tree of the Dead

At first glance, it's nothing more than a rather large, hulking tree in the middle of a cemetery. But it isn't until you see the other side that you begin to have doubts—and when you stare into the face of death. Well, battery death.

My first encounter with what I now call "The Tree of the Dead" occurred on a snowy January afternoon. My husband and I were taking photos in a cemetery in Terre Haute, Indiana, when he called me over to see the bizarre tree he had discovered. What appeared to be an ordinary old tree in fact had twisted limbs, odd burls, and a gapping, jagged cavity splitting open the trunk on the other side. It was the perfect "scary" tree, one I couldn't pass up a chance to photograph.

After walking to my chosen spot, I lifted the camera, aimed, clicked the button, and—nothing happened. I tried again, and the camera closed down. Turning it on again elicited the same response. Apparently the batteries were dead, even though I had just put new ones in ten minutes ago.

No big deal. There are a hundred reasons for camera batteries to die while on a trip: installation blunders, fluctuating temperatures, spirits draining batteries in order to manifest themselves. Regardless of which you choose to believe, batteries do lose charge quickly in a graveyard, so tombstone tourists always take extra.

After trekking back to the car for fresh batteries, I approached the tree again and the same thing happened—several more times. After yet another set of new batteries, I began having a "chat" with the tree. I wasn't pleased and apparently, the tree wasn't either. This would be a great photo for one of my cemetery presentations, and I was determined to get it. Hearing the one-sided conversation and deducing the problem, my husband arrived with his camera. Turning it on, he handed it to me and I was able to get two quick shots … before those batteries died as well.

Though I can't quite explain why the Tree of the Dead had such an aversion to having its picture taken (or what vendetta it had against my camera), the story stands as a lesson to all tombstone tourists: Always have a backup.

This picture took me several camera batteries to take.

Mind Your Safety

We tend to think of cemeteries as quiet, safe, peaceful vistas, but you may visit some that are remote, isolated, or in sketchy neighborhoods. Your personal safety should always come first. Consider taking a genealogy buddy with you. In addition to providing safety, a travel partner will also share the thrill of the discovery with you.

If you do go it alone, be aware. Although it's called "The City of the Dead," you still need to pay attention to where you are and what's going on around you, especially if you're in an unfamiliar neighborhood. Always carry a charged cell phone with you, and do not hesitate to call 911 if something or someone seems dangerous to you. In addition, if you are being followed, watched, or harassed, get safely back to your vehicle and leave. Then report the incident to the police and the cemetery office.

If you see signs of recent vandalism (or another concerning activity), leave the area and report it to the cemetery office. Also, keep anything of value out of sight in your vehicle and remember to lock the doors. It is always better to play it safe—even if you feel a bit ridiculous—than to end up sorry you didn't follow a warning hunch.

Learn the Lay of the Land

Once you've arrived at the cemetery, take a photo of the cemetery sign and any gates and buildings located at the entrance. This will help you keep your photographic records straight and provide you with a visual journal of your trip.

If there is a cemetery office, stop in and see what resources it offers. Check for maps, brochures, and any historical and notable burials. While you're there, ask if tours are offered, or if there is a self-service tour you can enjoy on your own time. Query office personnel about the general history of the cemetery. Many have cemetery history books for sale; some offer a simple handout. But all of that material gives you a better understanding of the area and the era when your ancestors lived there.

Take the time to make a general drive or walk through the cemetery before you get involved in your research. That way, you'll know the general layout and have a feel for your surroundings. Also, find out what the cemetery hours are and abide by them.

Image A: Wild animals often make their homes in cemeteries, so you'll need to keep an eye out for flora and fauna.

Pay Attention

As you survey the cemetery and make your way through it, watch for broken stones in your path, and make sure you don't lean on monuments or sit on stones. In addition to being disrespectful to the dead, doing so puts you at risk if there are weak spots in the marker that might give way to pressure. Also take care when backing up to take photos; sunken graves can literally take you off your feet. Be on the lookout for snakes, lizards, wasps, and other critters that make the cemetery their home (image **A**).

Be Skeptical

Remember, just because something is engraved in stone doesn't make it true. Although cemetery records can provide great information, they're also generally considered secondary sources. Take lots of photos, and always check against original, primary sources when you get home. The wrong number or letter can make a world of difference and alter your research. Carvers and informants can make gaffes, so treat gravestones just like any other genealogy source.

The gravestone in image **B** proves the point. The name was originally carved as *Lliam*, but someone has added a *WI* to indicate the gentleman's name was originally William. As a family researcher, this

Image B: Errors on tombstones can throw off your research. On this one, for example, the *WI* in William was added after the rest of the inscription. Was the deceased's name William, or Lliam?

4

opens up all kinds of research questions: What was his birth name? Did he drop the *WI* from his name? If so, why—were there too many Williams in the family? Was there a family feud so he wanted to distance himself from the other Williams? Think over some possibilities and start digging. The answer is out there; you just have to find out where. But thanks to this tombstone, you have more clues to follow.

Be Respectful

Treat everything with respect: the gravestones and monuments, the trees, grave plantings, and landscaping elements. If a funeral service is going on near your destination, reroute until it's over. Avoid doing anything that could damage the stones or grounds. Remember the tombstone tourist's Golden Rule: Take only photos—leave only footprints.

Have Fun!

Yes, you can enjoy yourself in a cemetery! Admire what's there. If the cemetery offers walking or driving tour maps, grab one and get going. Once your research is done, plan some time to just enjoy being outdoors. Photograph what you find interesting. You will be amazed at what you can uncover in a cemetery—exquisite artwork, interesting architecture, landscaped grounds, poems and prose, intrigue about the lives of history's rich and famous. You can make a day's worth of interesting and enjoyable pursuits with just a little planning.

TWENTY-ONE NUGGETS OF INFORMATION

Now that you've learned how to plan your trip and have some tips about navigating the cemetery itself, you'll need to know what information to keep an eye out for as you complete your field research. Here are twenty-one facts to find in the cemetery:

DATE OF DEATH

This is the actual date of the individual's death, not the date she was buried.

CAUSE OF DEATH

The immediate cause of death may be listed in a general way—aging, disease, accident, homicide, suicide—or in a very specific way—dropsy (swelling of the kidney or heart), flux (hemorrhage or diarrhea), a long sickness (tuberculosis), softening of the brain (stroke or hemorrhage in the brain), or milk fever (milk from cattle that ate poisonous plants.) RootsWeb has an impressive list of disease names used during the nineteenth century, which can be helpful when searching through family records <rootsweb.ancestry.com/~njmorris/general_info/disease. htm>. When you know what disease someone died of, you can take that information and compile a family medical history.

AGE AT DEATH

Birth years and ages are two gravemarker details that may be purposely incorrect. Without a valid way to check the exact year of someone's birth, many people took the opportunity to subtract a few years from their actual age. While it might have made Great-grandma feel better (and maybe even somewhat younger), it presents the family researcher with more details to check and verify.

FULL NAME, INCLUDING MAIDEN NAME

A person's full name, including the complete middle name or initial, may be inscribed on his headstone. It became more prevalent in the latter part of the twentieth century to list a woman's maiden name on her tombstone, but some stones from the late 1800s to mid 1900s may also show a woman's maiden name along with her married surname. Check other records to make sure the name isn't from a first marriage instead of being her birth name. A woman's odd-sounding "middle" name could actually be her maiden name, so check and see if it is a family surname.

DECEASED'S ADDRESS

What is listed as the deceased's final address may or may not be where he or she lived. Many times, older adults were taken in by family members and shuttled around. This could be the actual address where the deceased resided at the end of life or where he was living for the past few weeks or months. If the address doesn't coincide with your notes, investigate to see if the deceased had moved in with a grown child or grandchild. That, in turn, can give you even more information about the family.

LOCATION WHERE DEATH OCCURRED

Again, the location is where the death took place, not necessarily where the deceased lived. If she were visiting a family member in another part of the state when death occurred, this would be the location of death.

NAME OF ATTENDING PHYSICIAN OR HOSPITAL

On older forms, you may find the name of the attending physician and a notation that death occurred "at home." As we advanced into the twentieth century, more deaths occurred in hospitals, nursing homes, and hospice facilities.

COMPLETE BIRTH AND MARRIAGE DATES

Many times, birth and marriage certificates are included with the death certificate, making research on a certain individual much easier.

RELATIONSHIPS

The deceased's relationship to other family members can provide more information. If the deceased is listed as a mother or father, we can deduce they had children. If no children are mentioned later in the parent's lives, we might begin searching for children who died young, looking for epidemics that spread through the area at the time and searching for children's or infants' stones at the parents' grave plots.

NAME OF PLOT OWNER

Don't assume that the family purchased the plot where your ancestor is buried. Dig deeper and see whose name is listed as the owner of the grave lot. You might be surprised. Maybe the purchaser bought several plots at one time for the entire family, or a neighbor could have bought the plot, knowing that the deceased could not afford it. The stories can be varied, so be open to the possibilities.

4

COST OF THE BURIAL PLOT

The price of the grave may be listed on the burial form, along with other expenses incurred such as opening the grave, closing the grave, placing a vault, or setting a tombstone/monument.

COST OF THE FUNERAL AND/OR BURIAL

Funeral expenses have gone up tremendously in recent years, thanks to the host of options available to include in a funeral service and/or burial. Our ancestors also had numerous decisions to make. The local undertaker offered all types of services, such as providing extra chairs in the parlor to seat funeral attendees, placing newspaper announcements, notifying friends and other loved ones, providing funeral sashes, hiring music, arranging for the tolling of the bells in town, arranging for extra candles and flowers, providing a hearse to transport the deceased to the graveyard, adding extra adornments to the funeral hearse, preparing memorial cards with the deceased's favorite verse, locating extra horses to pull the hearse, and (generally only for the well-to-do) even hiring professional mourners. Funerals became a sort of parade, and those in the middle-to-upper classes were expected to show their social standing at a funeral with these extras.

DECEASED'S OCCUPATION

Discovering what your ancestor did for a living is always interesting and may bring about speculation and questions (e.g., Did anyone in the family continue down that path?). But many times we come across a term that has no valid meaning to us in the twenty-first century. For example, would you know what your relative did if the occupation listed was a *bauer* (farmer), *fogger* (peddler or low-class lawyer), *necessary woman* (maid who emptied chamber pots), *rectifier* (a distiller of alcoholic spirits), or *ship husband* (ship repairman)? RootsWeb offers a list of occupations that can assist you in figuring out what Great-great-great-grandpa really did <**www.rootsweb.ancestry.com/~usgwkidz/ oldjobs.htm**>. Also pay attention to symbols on a tombstone that might convey occupation (see chapter 6).

MILITARY SERVICE

Did your ancestor serve in a war or military conflict? First, check the headstone to see if a rank, unit, branch of service, or war was listed. Also look on the back of stones for military plaques. Many times, military service organizations placed a service or association emblem by the grave to signify a member—for example, a symbol of the American Legion or Grand Army of the Republic, indicating a Union soldier who served in and was honorably discharged from the Civil War.

FUNERAL AND MEMORIAL CARDS

Memorial cards have gone by several names over the years, including mourning cards, remembrance cards, and cabinet memorial cards. Whatever you call them, funeral cards date back to the mid-1800s and were sent out to family, friends, and neighbors to notify them of the date and time of the funeral or mass. If you received such a card, you were expected to attend the service; not to do so was considered rude.

During the Victorian era, memorial cards always included the deceased's name (many times, the full name), date of death, and age— sometimes listed by year, month, and day. A poem or specially selected verse would also be printed, along with a symbol or two that held religious significance for (or was otherwise important to) the deceased. The card was sent to far-off family and friends well after the funeral had taken place, and served as a keepsake to put in a photo album or the family Bible. A photo of the deceased, possibly taken after death, might be glued to the back of the card, especially if it was a child who had died. Locks of hair were also treasured items to include. Memorial cards were printed on black stock with gold trim during the 1800s, but white and gray card stock became popular with the new century. By the 1930s, with the tremendous changes in society, cabinet memorial cards became passé.

OBITUARY OR DEATH NOTICE

An obituary is a short write-up about the person who died, listing significant details about his life and where the funeral was to be held, including the date and time. Obituaries were usually published in newspapers throughout the area where the deceased lived. These life details can tell us something about the person that we may not have come across before.

A death notice is different from an obituary in that it does not include personal details, simply the date of death and funeral information.

COPY OF THE DEATH CERTIFICATE

Family researchers are always interested in death certificates because of the clues they contain. A death certificate will state the cause of death along with the birth date and, at times, a birthplace. A death certificate may be full of names for parents, spouses, and children, and it may also contain maiden names. The decedent's occupation may be mentioned, along with military status.

NOTES FROM PEOPLE (FUNERAL HOME STAFF, ATTENDING CLERGY, MONUMENT COMPANY, OR STONECARVER)

Each of these suggestions can lead to information you might not have discovered before. The funeral home may have been used several times by your family. Check with its staff and see if records contain other surnames you're searching for. Look for the name of the informant, such as a relative or neighbor. Also check for the names of other family members, and where the deceased was living, plus if the undertaker kept any physical folders that could have obituaries, memorial cards, or funeral programs tucked away in them.

Clergy can help locate the church your family attended. From there, check church records for information on marriages, births, burials, confirmations, communion services, Sunday school attendance lists, church newsletters, and church history books.

The name of the monument company can put you on the path to even more information, depending on what the company has in its files. Companies usually created work orders, which detailed who purchased the monument, whom it was for, what was selected, how much it cost, and where it was placed.

The stonecarver may work for the monument company, but local carvers may have created older tombstones. If you have the carver's name, you can learn who this person was and what type of work he did. Some stonecarvers were known throughout a region or state. In Bedford, Indiana, many of the carvers from the 1800s and early 1900s are still remembered, and the local historical society has information on several of them.

UNDERTAKER'S NAME

The undertaker, now called the funeral director, was the person who transferred the body from the home to the cemetery. The undertaker also dealt with the funeral arrangements, from locating a coffin and selecting the carriage to act as a hearse to hiring professional mourners and selling memorial cards. He was known as the "master of ceremonies." Many undertakers started out as livery or cabinetmakers and morphed into the trade during the mid-1800s.

GRAVE OPENING AND CLOSING ORDERS

These orders allowed the cemetery gravediggers to dig open the grave and, once the casket was placed in it, close or cover the grave. The orders can contain information not usually collected, such as the type of burial container, a description of the memorial or marker, name of the funeral home along with the address, next of kin, and name of the lot owner.

TYPE OF GRAVE

Your ancestors may have been buried in numerous types of graves:
- A single plot is one burial lot; a companion plot is large enough for two to be buried next to one another.
- A mausoleum is usually an ornate, freestanding structure that can hold the remains of an individual or a large family.
- A community mausoleum is open to anyone. Family mausoleums were one way to communicate a family's social status.
- Walled graves or wall vaults are graves located in walls—think of the cemeteries in New Orleans where flooding is an issue.
- Crypts, also referred to as catacombs, were usually located under churches, mainly in Europe.

RESPONSIBLY RECORDING HEADSTONE INFORMATION

There are many ways to keep a record of what is on a headstone, but the best is with a camera. Today, with high-quality digital cameras and smartphone cameras, there is no reason not to use this method to document your ancestor's headstone. It's easy to transpose a letter or number, and a camera gives you an instant image of what is there. But there are some tricks to getting good photos. Here are a few suggestions for photographing headstones as a way to record the information.

Make sure the headstone is clean and readable before you begin. Grab that cemetery bag we discussed earlier in this chapter and in chapter 3, and use those scissors to trim grass from around the stone. Dust off any dirt or grass and spray a light mist of water on the stone to make the letters stand out. If bird droppings are a problem, take a soft cloth and wet it before gently cleaning the stone.

Take a photo of the entire grave plot so you can see the full headstone and any plantings, trees, or other site markers near the grave.

Stones Can Tell a Story

This tall tree stone, an impressive monument that can be seen throughout the cemetery, marks the grave of twenty-seven-year-old Charles King. But when you move closer, you begin to see clues that help to unravel the story of how Charles died.

May 12, 1893, was a warm, rainy day in Jonesboro, Arkansas, and King was traveling aboard the St. Louis, Arkansas, and Texas Railway from Vincennes, Indiana—his hometown—to an unknown destination in the south. The details of what happened that day have been lost to time, but the story carved on this gravestone tells us that the train Charles King was riding derailed that day. King's body was sent back home to Indiana where he was buried in Greenlawn Cemetery. His parents were so distressed over his death that they had the story of the accident carved on the trunk of his tree stone grave marker, and at the bottom of the tree is a train engine and an overturned coal car, a visual reminder of how their son lost his life that warm spring day.

For King's descendants—and other tombstone tourists—the story is a memorable depiction of a tragedy that rocked a family and community.

The images on tombstones can tell elaborate stories about the deceased.

Zoom in to show the entire headstone, and take photos at eye level instead of shooting down on the stone.

Divide the headstone into sections, if it is large, and begin photographing from the top down. Zoom in on any symbols or markings. Get a good crisp shot of the names, dates, and any inscriptions. Once you have photographed the front of the stone, take pictures of the sides (if necessary) and the back (if the stone is vertical).

Do not move a stone for a better view; if it has a hairline crack, you could end up damaging it.

Develop a strategy for multiple tombstones. If there are two individual markers, as with a couple, photograph one and then the other, but be sure to get a shot of both stones in one photo. If there are several family members buried in an area, get a panoramic shot of the graves and begin at the upper left working toward the right and down, photographing each gravestone. (Always shooting in the same direction will help you remember how a section was laid out.) Begin photographing those markers surrounding the headstone of interest in a clockwise manner.

Photographing on a cloudy day can make the headstones easier to read. If the stone is in shadow or under a tree on a bright day, try using the flash on your camera to brighten it up. Take a mirror or aluminum foil and cardboard in case you need to bounce light onto the stone.

 ## KEYS from the CRYPT

• Create clear, defined goals for your cemetery trip. While simply walking around the cemetery can be fun and relaxing, you'll want to make sure you're making the most of your time there, particularly if the site is far from your home.

• Stop by the office before traveling too far into the cemetery. Offices might contain maps of the cemetery or gravesite directories, which can help reduce your research time. Also consider scheduling an appointment with cemetery officials or local historical or genealogical society members.

• Note everything about the tombstones, and be on the lookout for other kinds of records that are available in cemeteries (see chapter 2).

• Refrain from recording tombstones in any way but picture form. Other recording methods can damage stones.

Reading Headstones

Recording information on gravestones has been popular for centuries. In addition to their beauty and cultural significance, tombstones provide historical information valuable to history buffs and genealogists alike. As a result, genealogists love to have a physical record of an ancestor's tombstone. In the mid-twentieth century, making tombstone rubbings was a favorite family activity as everyone learned about genealogy. But time, weather, and even the most careful tombstone-rubbing can take their toll on a stone.

Given that, the best and most accurate way to record gravestone inscriptions is with a camera. With digital cameras, and now smartphone cameras, you can easily record your ancestor's tombstone for posterity, without having to resort to other methods that can damage headstones (such as tombstone rubbings).

In this chapter, we'll discuss some strategies for photographing old tombstones, plus how to overcome reading difficulties caused by erosion, weathering, and old-style handwriting.

STRATEGIES FOR (SAFELY) ENHANCING WRITING ON TOMBSTONES

Many markers from the eighteenth and nineteenth centuries are difficult to read, due, in part, to the types of stone that were used. Sand-

Image A: Weathering can take a serious toll on tombstones. Tombstone tourists can use tricks to decipher tombstone writing.

stone and limestone do not stand up well to the elements, which slowly destroy the stone as it crumbles and flakes away. Inscriptions become worn and slowly erode until the lettering is unreadable (image **A**).

Over the years, genealogists have devised several methods to enhance reading stones, but many of those have now been discarded as too damaging to the markers. However, genealogists and other tombstone tourists still have a few tricks in their arsenal for improving inscriptions' legibility.

The best tool I've found for reading faded lettering is a spray bottle filled with water. By (lightly) spraying the epitaph on stones with only light wear, you can darken the stone and make the letters more distinct and easier to read. You'll have a tougher time working with stones that are almost worn smooth, but the next suggestion may work best.

Harnessing sunlight may also help make the lettering on the stones more readable, so carry a small 8x10 mirror in a sturdy frame to redirect light onto the stone. By angling the mirror to reflect sunlight on the stone, you can highlight the lettering and make it easier to read. Continue to angle the mirror so you can photograph the sides and back of the stone, if need be. If you're running out of room in your cemetery bag, you can also use a small compact mirror. While it won't provide light on a large area, smaller mirrors can still make the letters in the reflected section stand out.

If you're at the cemetery and are short a mirror (or worry about breaking one), aluminum foil also makes a good light reflector. Take a length of foil and wrap it around a piece of cardboard. Then hold or prop it up at the correct angle so the light bounces onto the front of the stone, making the inscription easier to read and photograph.

TOMBSTONE WEATHERING

Tombstones are expected to last for centuries, but unfortunately the weather and elements slowly erode and destroy them. Cemeteries face different degrees of weathering based on the climate in which they reside.

Two of the most significant factors affecting how (and how quickly) tombstones erode are the type of stone and the stone's location. A cemetery located on a seacoast or in a semi-arid or cold desert region, for example, will have stones damaged by "salt weathering," a physical type of weathering that occurs when saline gets into cracks and pores of a tombstone. The results are flaking and crumbling. Another location-

Preservation Techniques You Should Lay to Rest

Taking rubbings from gravestones was popular during the twentieth century, but today we know that it's damaging to the marker. Handling older stones puts unnecessary pressure on them, which can result in hairline cracks that will eventually break. The actual process of the rubbing is also abrasive to the marker, and using charcoal or chalk can cause permanent deterioration due to scratching and leaving a colored residue that does not wash off in the rain.

Other unacceptable techniques include flour, talc, and cornstarch. All will penetrate cracks and crevices in a stone, and those gaps, once wet, will swell and enlarge the hairline fractures. These products also encourage the growth of lichens, mold, and other invasive vegetation on grave markers.

Shaving cream is definitely off limits to family historians. Composed of several chemicals, shaving cream acts similar to acid rain and will eventually destroy a stone.

Image B: Cracks can form in tombstones as the temperature fluctuates, causing the stone to expand and contract, and enlargening any existing faults.

related problem involves the direction the tombstone faces. In the United States, a north–facing grave marker will show more weathering than stones facing other directions, as harsh winter weather blows in from the north and west. See the Types of Gravestones sidebar late in this chapter for more on how a gravestone's material makeup can affect how it becomes damaged.

There are three types of weathering that effect stone monuments:

- **Physical weathering:** This refers to damages caused by the elements, including precipitation, temperature changes, and wind. For example, expansion-contraction weathering (one kind of physical weathering) occurs when a stone warms up during the day, then rapidly cools at night. Similar temperature variations occur during the spring and autumn seasons in temperate climates, along with desert locations where temperatures fluctuate from extreme highs during the day to dramatic lows at night. Similarly, during "freeze-thaw" (image **B**), temperatures hover around the freezing point, fluctuating back and forth between freezing and thawing. Any moisture in the stone's joints, cracks, or pores freezes then thaws rapidly. As water freezes, it expands, creates spalling (a type of flaking) on the marker, which can break or create a larger crack. This causes any gaps to widen and the stone to become unstable, possibly falling and breaking. Sandstone and limestone markers are particularly subject to this effect, as are marble headstones once water gets into their cracks and joints.

- **Biological weathering:** This refers to damage done by non-human organisms. For example, lichen, mold, or algae often grow on stones (image **C**), causing damage to the underlying stone and making inscriptions difficult to read. Ivy, another growth that is prevalent in the cemetery, has suckers that attach to stones and cause damage. Gravestones near plant roots (such as those of a tree) are especially prone to biological weathering, as the acid secreted by the plant's roots damage the marker. Tree roots can also move stones, causing them to topple or overturn.

- **Chemical weathering:** Chemical weathering occurs when the minerals in the stone are altered, changing the tombstone's surface and even decomposing it altogether (image **D**). Acid rain is a major contributor to chemical weathering and affects all gravestones in some manner. For example, sandstone graves that have an orange or yellowish cast are already showing signs of oxidation (a result of acid rain), and acid rain also affects granite grave markers (which generally seem to be weatherproof) by wearing away at the stone's joints where water comes in contact with the feldspar mineral in the stone.

Weathering Versus Erosion

While some people may use the terms "weathering" and "erosion" interchangeably, the two processes affect stones in slightly different ways. Weathering occurs when a rock breaks down due to the temporary or intermittent effects of the local climate, whereas erosion results from some type of more active abrasion. For example, a tombstone experiencing weathering might gradually lose its shape and definition as rain and wind affect it off and on, but erosion occurs when water rushes over river rocks for decades. The two processes can work together, however: Melting snow (a temporary, weather-related factor) may melt across the front of a cemetery stone, removing flakes and chips that are then carried away in erosion.

Image C: Biological weathering occurs when organisms like algae or lichen grow on stones.

Image D: Chemical substances like acid rain can seriously damage headstones.

Tombstone tourists *can* help reverse weathering processes, but you should always take precautions when attempting to do so. Know what type of stone you want to clean, as not every method or product works on every type of grave marker. Chemical processes can deter the effects of weathering and biological growth on some stones, but you can't simply buy something and apply it to any stone. Before you consider chemicals advertised to clean off lichen or mold, try using water and a very soft bristled brush to gently wipe—not scrub—the growth away.

If removing growth requires more elbow grease (or if you don't want to take a chance handling a damaged stone), contact a local cemetery sexton for advice. Sextons go to cemetery conferences around the world and should know some of the best (and safest) techniques being used today. You might also check a state university to find out what studies on reversing weathering effects on stones have yielded, or check in with art conservators who might know how to handle tombstones. (Yes—these gravestones are pieces of art!)

Types of Gravestones

Researchers can expect to find six major kinds of stones that were used as tombstones:

Fieldstones (1600s–present) were the earliest type of stone or rock used to mark graves due to their abundance. Also called non-quarried stones, these were durable and could be carved or chiseled with a design or lettering.

Slate (1600s–1900s) is found mainly in the eastern United States. Boston produced most of the Early American gravestones crafted from this hallmark gray stone. Slate can withstand freeze-thaw (physical) weathering fairly well and doesn't appear to be much affected by acid rain. However, slate's porousness makes it subject to delamination (the separating of the stone into layers). Slate is still used today in some regions.

Sandstone (1650s–late 1800s) was popular because of its availability and ease of carving. Sandstone can range in color from red to light tan to brown. Spalling or flaking, in which pieces of the stone become detached, can damage the stone, sometimes in small quantities like chips of paint, and sometimes in sheets (delamination). Lichen and mold then begin to grow between the stone and the raised-up flaking piece. As the flakes fall off, the stone's surface becomes uneven and begins to wear away.

Limestone (mid-1700s–1930s) was much-favored in the Midwest, where you could find an abundance of it during the mid-1800s to 1900s. Limestone is easy to carve and ranges in color from light brown to pure white. Limestone is terribly affected by severe weather conditions. Acid rain can cause extreme damage to a limestone marker, causing pitting—depressions that show on the surface of the stone.

Marble (1780s–1930s) has been used for centuries to build monuments due to its strength and appealing appearance. Marble is usually white with bluish or grayish veins running through it. Despite its strength and beauty, marble can also deteriorate, mainly from acid rainfall that causes the surface of the marble to appear and feel grainy. As acid rain takes its toll, the stone's lettering begins to lose its sharpness and slowly fades away.

Granite (mid-1800s–present) is one of the most durable options for gravestones, and is the preferred tombstone type used today. In fact, there are many cemeteries today that *only* allow granite stones and monuments to be erected. Granite does not erode, and (for the most part) is resistant to deterioration. Granite was once difficult to carve and required skilled stonecarvers, but modern techniques make it much easier to carve. However, granite is not impregnable; deterioration caused by the effects of acid rain usually begins with the lettering on the stone, which erodes and loses its definition.

Fieldstone

Slate

Sandstone

Limestone

Marble

Granite

GRAVE MARKER GUIDE

Cemetery markers have changed through the years, from the minimally decorated stones of the eighteenth and early nineteenth centuries to those elaborate Victorian mausoleum and monument showpieces of the mid-to-late 1800s. The early twentieth century was a treasure trove of shapes and styles, including new types of markers such as white bronze and tree stones.

Here are some of the most common types of grave markers:

BEVEL MARKER

A bevel marker, also known as a pillow marker, is a stone that lies flat on the ground with a slightly sloped front and pitched rock edges.

FLAT MARKER

Also called a lawn marker, flush marker, or grass marker, this kind of marker is level with the ground. Flat markers are usually the smallest gravestones that can be purchased. Names and dates are carved on the marker, which might include a small design or border.

LEDGER MARKER

A full-sized ledger stone covers the entire grave; a half ledger covers half of the grave. Ledger markers can be made of sandstone, marble, bronze, or granite.

OBELISK

An obelisk monument is a vertical marker with four sides that get narrower as it increases in height, ending with a pointed top. This style of headstone originated in Egypt as a tribute to the sun god Ra, and became popular in the United States in the mid-1800s.

SARCOPHAGUS

A sarcophagus (from the Greek, meaning "flesh consuming") is hollow inside in order to hold a body or a coffin, then a lid or cover piece is placed on the top. Today a sarcophagus is symbolic, with the body

Bevel marker

Flat marker

Obelisk

Ledger marker

Sarcophagus

5

Slant marker

Tablet marker

Tree stone marker

White bronze marker

buried in the ground underneath the monument rather than directly within it. The oldest known sarcophagi are from Egypt.

SLANT MARKER

The front of a slant marker, where the information and inscription are placed, slopes toward the back of the stone. A slant headstone sits upright on a concrete or granite base, giving the impression of a more expensive stone. It is usually carved from granite with a flat top.

TABLET MARKER

A tablet stone is an upright monument placed on top of a base. These markers can differ greatly in shape and size. A single tablet stone is usually taller than it is wide, while a double or companion tablet stone will be wider than it is tall.

TREE STONE MARKER

A tree-shaped gravestone is known as a tree stone, tree trunk, or tree stump marker. Popular from the 1880s to the 1920s, tree stones vary in size and height, from tiny children's stones to soaring tree monuments up to ten or twelve feet tall. Almost all have intricate carvings that make these markers unique.

WHITE BRONZE MARKER

White bronze markers were popular from the 1870s to 1910, when some people considered marble and granite too expensive to be used for gravestones. Despite the name, white bronze markers are actually 99-percent zinc. These monuments (now bluish-gray due to oxidation) ranged in size from just a foot tall to more than twenty-five feet high. Families could select from pre-cast panels that depicted imagery indicating something of interest to the deceased. White bronze gravestones are extremely durable, and most have survived into this century. Unfortunately, white bronze markers fell out of favor when people began opting for the more expensive granite.

READING OLD SCRIPT

Imagine—you've found the cemetery where your ancestor is buried, traveled to the town, met and talked with several groups, and read through the forms and talked with the cemetery sexton. Then, as you approach your ancestor's final resting place, you see it—the gravestone, not covered with lichens or mold or clinging ivy. What luck! You slowly walk toward the stone, eager to read the veritable goldmine of information on its face … and see the handwriting is almost impossible to read (image **E**). What do you do?

Hard-to-read script can be a real buzzkill, but there are plenty of ways to decode archaic fonts and handwriting. Photograph and transcribe exactly what you see on the stone—don't assume or guess at what a letter is. Take everything literally to start, no matter how confusing. Then, highlight the words or letters that are hard to read.

One problem is that several letters can be hard to distinguish from one another on stones and in handwritten documents. The letter *S* could also look like an *f* or *p,* and two *S*'s in a row would be written differently to discern them. (Tricky, I know.) Another letter that caused problems was the letter *I,* as it could be written as *I, i, l* or *j. L* and *J* provide similar difficulties. Other letters that look alike in older handwriting include the lower case *b* and *f, k* and *t, d* and *el, w* and *u* or *uu, w* and *v* or *vv.* Likewise, *y* could be confused for *g* or *q.*

When you're dealing with upper case letters, watch out for *F* and *H, K* and *R, O* and *Q, P* and *R, U* and *V,* and *W* (which could be confused with an *M, UU* or *VV*).

For help, look for information on the time period and language that the stone was carved in. Find someone at a local university who teaches that language, or search for people who transcribe text regularly. Also look for folks at museums and historical societies who can handle the challenge, thanks to work with paleography and hard-to-read handwriting on old forms and in books.

In addition to struggling to decipher letters, many genealogists also struggle with inscriptions written in Old English, Gothic, or Black Lettering fonts. These scripts were popular in Western Europe from the Middle

Image E: This tombstone is hard to read due to both its weathering and its indecipherable script.

Ages through the seventeenth century. Locating an expert in this area can make the process much easier.

You can also find excellent online resources for understanding old script. Here are a few to get started:

- Brigham Young University (BYU) Script Tutorial <**script.byu.edu/Pages/home.aspx**>
- English Handwriting 1500–1700 online course <**www.english.cam.ac.uk/ceres/ehoc/lessons.html**>
- Jewish Records Indexing—Poland Transliteration Standards <**jri-poland.org/translit.htm**>
- Omniglot: Gothic <**www.omniglot.com/writing/gothic.htm**>
- The National Archives Paleography: Reading Old Handwriting <**www.nationalarchives.gov.uk/palaeography**>

 ## KEYS from the CRYPT

• Refrain from creating tombstone rubbings or using other methods of recording tombstone inscriptions. Taking photographs (and digitally enhancing them later) will record most of the information you'll need.

• Learn to identify the different kinds of tombstones and the materials used to make them, as these can give you clues about your ancestor's community and socioeconomic status.

Headstone Iconography Guide

For thousands of years, humans have used symbols to convey their thoughts, feelings, and desires to others. In the mid-1800s, symbolism became popular on gravestones as more ornate and detailed symbols were used not only to record facts, but also to tell a story about the deceased's life. Symbols were a way to honor a loved one and also provide comfort to those left behind. For more than eighty years from 1839 to 1920, symbols and icons were used as a silent language that shared clues about the deceased and his beliefs. Symbolism also made it easier for those who couldn't read to get the gist of what was being "said" on a gravestone. Several symbols can adorn a single stone and offer layers of meanings, providing a glimpse into the deceased's life, interests, and fears.

The Victorians, who had a large impact on gravestone décor, loved a good secret. In fact, they had secret meanings assigned to all kinds of things such as colors, flowers, and birds (image **A**). It's no wonder the cemetery is full of Victorian symbolism and that grave symbols contain secret messages.

In this chapter, we'll discuss how to identify and interpret the most common symbols that appear on gravestones.

Image A: The symbols and inscriptions on tombstones can contain hidden meanings.

A HISTORY OF US CEMETERY SYMBOLS

Although it is difficult to pinpoint when certain symbols began to be used, we know that early and Colonial Americans decorated their tombstones with death's heads, skulls, crossbones, hourglasses, and scythes (image **B**)—all to indicate the passing of time and the mortality of man. But, unlike today, tombstone symbols were not used to bring a measure of comfort and hope to the grieving. Instead they were used to instill the "fear of God" in those left behind so they would adhere to a more chaste and moral life.

By the early eighteenth century, our forefathers began to carve other symbols on the stones of their dead. Skulls and crossbones were still popular, as were a crossed spade and shovel (indicating death), the Grim Reaper (death personified), and an hourglass with wings to indicate that time flies. But other, more life-affirming symbols also began to appear: Willow trees indicated grief and mourning, winged cherubs depicted the flight of the soul, and an occasional dove offered hope to those in mourning of the ascent of the soul into heaven.

Image C: The Victorian era brought elaborate tombstone imagery, such as this tree trunk grave featuring an anchor.

Image B: Early gravestones had morbid symbols: an hourglass to symbolize passing time (right) and skull and crossbones to symbolize death (center).

6

During the nineteenth century, iconography became fashionable, with most gravestones bearing some icon or carving. Since the Victorians loved to tell stories, the symbols shed light on the deceased's life—at least the interesting parts. Suddenly, the cemetery was blossoming with carved flowers and vines, animals and birds, broken chains, and fraternal emblems that all told a story on stone. Ornate sculptures and architecture were part of the attraction of the rural cemeteries of the era: stately mausoleums with expensive stained glass windows, towering obelisks that bore down on the graves, and lifelike statues that took it all in (image **C**). The heavy use of symbols continued into the twentieth century until the Great Depression of the 1930s brought ostentatiousness to an end.

The mid-twentieth century bore little resemblance to the Victorian era. Gone were the massive, highly decorated grave markers. Stones

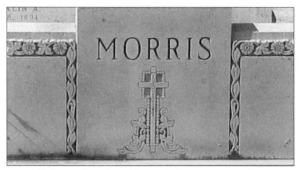

Image D: Stones from the mid-twentieth century were often austere, featuring little imagery or pageantry.

Image E: Nowadays, modern stonecutting techniques allow for more personal inscriptions, such as this one for a motorcycle lover.

were now low to the ground with few details besides dates, a name, and a few designs or decorations (image **D**). The age of extravagance had passed, taking with it part of the cemetery's beauty.

Today, thanks to computers and laser designs, cemetery stones again tell a story about the deceased, albeit not nearly as individualistic as those from an earlier time. Walk through a cemetery now, and you'll find stones with tractors, motorcycles (image **E**), cars, houses, and farms, along with couples strolling hand-in-hand into the sunset—all carved into the marker with lasers. Yes, they are better than the plain rectangular stones of the mid-century, but somehow they're still lacking that element of mystery and romance that was such a sublime part of cemeteries from the 1860s to 1920s.

The Legend of Stiffy Green

John Henkl was getting on in years. He had once been a successful business-man in the river town of Terre Haute, Indiana, but now he preferred spending his days strolling the downtown streets, smoking his pipe, and stopping to chat with friends and acquaintances. Always at his side was his devoted companion, a little bulldog named Stiffy Green for his wide, stiff gait and unusual green eyes.

New Years Eve, 1920, brought grief and sadness to the Henkl household: John Henkl had died. Stiffy was inconsolable. The bulldog sat by the coffin during the funeral. He followed the procession of cars to the cemetery, and once the mausoleum doors had been closed and locked, Stiffy took up his position on the front steps, acting as a guard and keeping watch over his beloved master. Family and friends traveled to the cemetery in bitterly cold temperatures, blinding snow, and icy weather to take Stiffy home. But Stiffy was persistent: He waited for his chance to slip out of the house during the night and would be found sitting on the steps outside his master's tomb the next morning.

John Henkl and his dog Stiffy are said to be heard walking around the cemetery at night.

The ever-faithful Stiffy Green lives on in another form inside his owner's mausoleum.

It wasn't long before Stiffy refused to eat or drink, and eventually he died outside those mausoleum doors. The family, feeling Stiffy had been such a loyal friend, figured the dog deserved to keep watch over Mr. Henkl in death as he had in life. He was sent to a taxidermist and placed inside the mausoleum, reunited once again with his dear master.

But soon there were reports among the cemetery staff that Stiffy had been moved inside the mausoleum. No one knew who could have done it, and other rumors claimed Stiffy regularly changed positions in the tomb. Then began the tales among cemetery workers who had heard a small dog barking near the Henkl Mausoleum about sunset and smelled Mr. Henkl's favorite pipe tobacco wafting in the air.

Slowly the rumors spread. Kids frequented the cemetery, daring each other to run up to the doors to see if Stiffy had moved. The situation grew out of control when someone took a gun to the mausoleum and shot out Stiffy's right eye. The cemetery requested that John Henkl's favorite companion be removed from the grounds; the family found a willing home for him at the Vigo County Historical Society.

The Terre Haute Lions Club then stepped in and had a replica of the Henkl Mausoleum built in the basement of the building. Stiffy was placed inside to resume his rightful place guarding his master's mausoleum.

But even today there are reports that just about dusk on quiet evenings you can hear a man's low voice and the joyous barking of a little dog. And, as the shadows lengthen, you might catch the smell of that rich pipe tobacco drifting through the air as John Henkl and Stiffy enjoy another evening stroll together ...

6

CATEGORIES OF SYMBOLS

Symbols generally mean different things to different people, but certain icons have more universal meanings in the context of headstones. Here are some of the more common meanings behind broad categories of symbols. For a more complete list, see the cemetery symbol quick guide at the end of the chapter.

Flowers

Flowers depicted the frailty of life and were placed on the stones of children and women (image **F**). Specific kinds of flowers also had their own meaning. Daffodils, for example, stood for grace, beauty, and a "deep regard" (i.e., affection).

A rose, the "Queen of the flowers," represents love, beauty, and virtue, while two intertwined roses symbolized a couple or a strong bond. A rosebud marked the grave of a child; a rose budding open indicated someone who had died young, never having blossomed. A rose in full bloom represented someone taken in the prime of life (image **G**). If a rose stem was broken, it indicated a life cut short (image **H**).

Image G: Roses in full bloom symbolized someone dying in the prime of life.

Image F: Flowers often represented the frailty of life, but certain flowers had additional meanings.

Lilies were majestic flowers that had as many meanings as there were types (image **I**):

- Easter lilies (or Madonna lilies) symbolized innocence, purity, and the resurrection.
- Calla lilies represented marriage and fidelity.
- Lily of the Valley, representing innocence and humility, was a favorite to place on the stone of someone who had died young.

Image H: Roses with broken stems symbolized a life cut short.

Image I: Lilies could represent many things, including innocence and humility.

The Victorians loved other kinds of greenery as well. Evergreen shrubs and vines symbolized faithfulness and everlasting remembrance, while ivy (image **J**), eternally green, represented faithfulness, a deep attachment, and undying affection.

Ferns are found growing deep in the woods, so Victorians placed them at the bottom of tree stones to represent sincerity, humility, and solitude (image **K**). A palm (image **L**), a reference to Palm Sunday, indicates the triumph over death via resurrection.

Trees and foliage, specifically, are carved on gravestones to indicate that life is ever changing. The type of tree depicted alters the meaning of the symbol. An oak leaf (image **M**), for example, stood for strength, stability, and endurance, and is usually found on an older man's grave; likewise, acorns indicated prosperity, power, and a triumph of the spirit. Broken trees, like roses (image **N**), with broken stems, could represent life cut short, often for men. Weeping willow trees (so named because they appear to be bent over in grief) were one of the first "cheerful" symbols used by Colonial Americans after abandoning the death's head, and they symbolize sorrow, mourning, and immortality.

6

Image J: Ivy, pictured here on a stone cross grave, was considered evergreen and represented faithfulness and undying affection.

GRAVE TIP

Follow Fraternity: The Modern Woodmen of America or Woodmen of the World, two fraternal organizations for woodworkers, created distinctive tree-shaped grave markers for members. If your ancestor is buried beneath one of these tree stones, he may have been a member of one of these organizations, so be on the lookout for membership documents and other records.

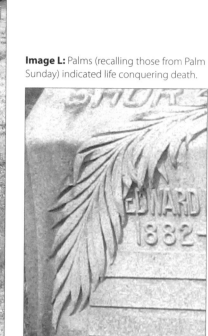

Image L: Palms (recalling those from Palm Sunday) indicated life conquering death.

Image K: Ferns on the base of tree stones harkened back to the solitude of the deep forest.

Images M: Oak leaves, such as the ones on these tombstones, stood for strength and endurance.

Image N: Like broken roses, broken trees could represent a life cut short.

Animals are abundant on cemetery stones. The lamb, found on the graves of children (image **O**), is the most popular cemetery symbol, representing innocence, purity, and gentleness. You may find two, three, or four together or side-by-side, representing how many children a family had lost.

Man's best friend, the dog, can be found in many guises throughout the graveyard. You can find family plots where a dog statue has been posted to guard the family (image **P**). A dog's love and devotion is often celebrated in the cemetery; search enough stones, and you'll discover a tombstone where a dog was incorporated into the carving, indicating this was a person worthy of unconditional love.

The lion is a symbolic guardian of the cemetery. These stone sentinels represented courage, honor, and power, and usually appear in pairs with one asleep and the other watchfully guarding the grave (image **Q**). Egyptian sphinxes were popular during the Neo-Egyptian era of the 1920s and may be used instead of lions. Sphinxes (image **R**) may be paired as a male and female, or two males may patrol the front of a tomb.

Birds are symbolic for the flight of the soul. Doves can be found on the graves of children and young adults, and they stand for peace, purity, and innocence (image **S**). An eagle represented power, courage in battle, and a military career. Eagles with wings outstretched are usually carved to stand upon Civil War monuments (image **T**).

Image O: Lambs often represented youth and adorned the graves of children.

Image P: Dogs sometimes served as sentries for their owners' graves.

Image Q: Lions represented courage and honor, and were often stationed outside graves.

Image R: Sphinxes served many of the same functions as lions, guarding graves.

6

Image S: Doves represented peace and innocence.

Image T: Eagles indicated power and a military career.

Besides the eagle, numerous images can represent a military career, including flags, an actual photo of the deceased dressed in a military uniform (image **U**), or specific letters that stand for a military group. *G.A.R.* inscribed on a stone, for example, stands for the "Grand Army of the Republic," indicating the deceased was a Union soldier in the Civil War, honorably discharged. Confederate graves may bear the southern flag of the Confederacy and the letters *C.S.A.*, which stands for the "Confederate States of America."

Actual cannons, artillery guns, cannonballs, and tanks have also been placed in local military cemeteries to symbolize war. Statues of the deceased in uniform may also stand by the graveside. For example, Private George Furr (age twenty-one) was killed while fighting with the 353rd Infantry, 4th Division. His parents paid honor to his memory by having an Italian stonecarver recreate George's likeness in Italian white cara marble. His statue (image **V**) stands today next to his grave on a hilltop overlooking Glenwood Cemetery in Shelbyville, Illinois.

6

Image U: Some military graves included a photo of the deceased in uniform.

Image V: Statues bearing a soldier's likeness were sometimes placed next to his grave.

Religious beliefs and affiliations are also denoted by special symbols and images. These can include a variety of crosses (including Latin, Greek, and Celtic; image **W**), praying hands, heavenly gates, an open or closed book, a chalice, or a crown. A crescent represents Islam, while a menorah or a Star of David represents Judaism. Angels and cherubs (image **X**) signify spirituality and rebirth.

Other religious symbols can be more dramatic. The stunning cemetery statue in image **Y**, from Kentucky, is of the warrior archangel

Image W: Crosses in various styles represented Christianity.

Image X: Cherubs, the short pudgy or childlike angels, represented spirituality and rebirth.

Image Y: Religious imagery, such as this statue of the archangel Michael crushing a demon, often appeared on a memorial.

Image Z: Your ancestor's occupation may have been indicated on his tombstone with symbols, such as this farmer, horse, and plow on a farmer's grave.

Michael, identifiable by his sword. The demon being crushed under Michael's boot represents Satan losing, once again, his fight against good.

Numerous symbols can indicate another key aspect of your ancestor's life and identity: trades and occupations. Some are easy to decipher, while others are a bit ambiguous. Here are just a few symbols for certain jobs and trades:

- Blacksmith: Anvil and hammer
- Butcher: Axe, knife sharpener, and cleaver
- Farmer: Plow, hoe, rack, stalk of corn, shock of wheat (image **Z**)
- Lawyer or court justice: Scales of justice
- Mariner: Anchor or sextant
- Weaver: Loom

KEYS from the CRYPT

• Note carefully any and all symbols that appear on your ancestor's tombstone. In addition to names, dates, and relationships, tombstones often have abstract symbols that indicate virtues (flowers, animals, birds, angels, trees) or more concrete icons that can lead you to other records (military insignias, religious icons, and occupational symbols).

• Research any abbreviations that appear on tombstones, as these can indicate membership in fraternal organizations, military organizations such as regiments, or other societies.

• Use tombstone symbols as starting points for further research to learn about the deceased's religion and occupation.

Cemetery Symbol Quick Guide

Type of symbol	Meaning
acorn	prosperity; power; triumph of the spirit
angel	rest/protection in the afterlife; spirituality; grief/mourning (when laying flowers on a grave)
baby	youth; innocence; new life
basket	fertility; maternal body
bird	flight of the soul
book	spirituality; scholarship
candle	life
cannon/ cannonball	military service
chalice	spirituality
clock	march of time; sometime displaying the time of death
column, broken	life cut short; sudden death
crescent	Islam
cross	Christianity
daffodil	grace; beauty; "deep regard"/affection
dog	unconditional love; devotion; loyalty
dove	peace; purity; innocence; death of a child or young adult
eagle	power; courage in battle; military career
evergreen shrub	faithfulness; remembrance
fern	sincerity; humility; solitude
flag	military service
flower	frailty of life; beauty
fruit	eternal plenty
foliage	changing nature of life
gun	military service

6

Type of symbol	Meaning
hands, praying	spirituality
heart	affection; marriage or love (when two hearts are joined)
hourglass	march of time
ivy	faithfulness; deep attachment; undying affection
key	knowledge; entrance into heaven
lamb	innocence; purity; gentleness; death of a child
lamp	knowledge; spiritual immortality
lion	courage; honor; power
lily	innocence and purity/the resurrection (Easter lilies); marriage and fidelity (calla lilies); innocence and humility, particularly of one who died young (Lily of the Valley)
menorah	Judaism
oak leaf	strength; stability; endurance
olive tree	peace; reconciliation between God and man
palm	triumph over death/resurrection
phoenix	resurrection
pillar, broken	life cut short; sudden death
rose	love; beauty; virtue; strong bond (when two roses are intertwined); dying in youth (as a rosebud or presented when budding)
skull	(with or without crossbones or wings) death
sphinx	courage; honor; power
tree	changing nature of life
tree stump	life cut short
urn	death
vine	faithfulness; remembrance
weeping willow	sorrow; mourning; immortality

6

Common Abbreviations and Meanings

Gravestone abbreviations offer insight into the deceased's life and interests. For example, fraternal organizations are often specified on gravestones, and this information can lead you to further record searches within these groups. Military service is identified by listing the unit served in or rank held.

AAONMS	Ancient Arabic Order of the Nobles of the Mystic Shrine (Shriners)
AASR	Ancient and Accepted Scottish Rite (Masonic)
AMORC	Ancient and Mystical Order Rosae Crucis (Rosicrucians)
AOH	Ancient Order of Hibernians (Catholic)
AOKMC	Ancient Order Knights of the Mystic Chain (Masonic)
AOUW	Ancient Order of United Workmen
BBG	Brevet Brigadier General
BGEN	Brigadier General
BLE	Brotherhood of Locomotive Engineers
BMG	Brigadier Major General
BPOE	Benevolent and Protective Order of Elks
CDR	Commander
COL	Colonel
CPL	Corporal
CPT	Captain
CSA	Confederate States of America
CSGT	Commissary Sergeant
DAR	Daughters of the American Revolution

EBA	Emerald Beneficial Association (Irish)
ENS	Ensign
FOE	Fraternal Order of Eagles
FOF	Fraternal Order of Firefighters
FOP	Fraternal Order of Police
GAR	Grand Army of the Republic
GEN	General
IOF	Independent Order of Foresters
IOJD	Independent Order of Job's Daughters (Masonic)
IOKP	Independent Order of Knights of Pythias
IOOF	Independent Order of Odd Fellows
IORG	Independent Order of the Rainbow for Girls (Masonic)
IORM	Independent Order of Red Men (Sons of Liberty)
ISH	Independent Sons of Honor (Masonic)
IUOM	Independent United Order of Mechanics
IWW	Industrial Workers of the World

6

K of C	Knights of Columbus (Catholic)		OGC	Order of the Golden Cross
KGE	Knights of the Golden Eagle		OSC	Order of the Scottish Clans
KHC	Knights of the Holy Cross (Catholic)		OSGT	Ordnance Sergeant
K of P	Knights of Pythias		PFC	Private First Class
KT	Knights Templar (Masonic)		PVT	Private
			QM	Quarter Master
LCDR	Lieutenant Commander		QMSGT	Quarter Master Sergeant
LGAR	Ladies of the Grand Army of the Republic		SAR	Sons of the American Revolution
LGEN	Lieutenant General		SGM	Sergeant Major
LOM	Loyal Order of Moose		SGT	Sergeant
LT	Lieutenant		SOT	Sons of Temperance
1 LT	First Lieutenant		SPC	Specialist
LTC	Lieutenant Colonel		SR	Scottish Rite (Masonic)
MAJ	Major		UCV	United Confederate Veterans
MGEN	Major General		UDC	United Daughters of the Confederacy
MWA	Modern Woodmen of America		VFW	Veterans of Foreign Wars
NCO	Non-commissioned Officer		WCTU	Woman's Christian Temperance Union
NOW	Neighbors of Woodcraft		WO	Warrant Officer
NSDAR	National Society of the Daughters of the American Revolution		WOW	Women of Woodcraft
			WOW	Woodmen of the World
OES	Order of the Eastern Star (Masonic)			

6

PART THREE

MAKING SENSE OF YOUR RESEARCH

Next Steps

eaving the cemetery with a huge amount of new information is always exciting, but what do you do once you get home? Figuring out what to do with all your hard-earned research—and how to make it fit with your pre-existing work—can be a challenge. You'll have to decide how to rectify conflicting facts, plus how the puzzle of your research fits together.

This chapter will discuss what to do after you return from the cemetery, with tips for incorporating your findings into genealogical research, a guide for touching up tombstone photos, and case studies that put all these ideas together to show cemetery research in action.

POST-TRIP TIPS

You've set down your cemetery bag, dusted off your shoes, and finally collapsed into your favorite armchair. So what comes next?

Begin by organizing what you've brought back. Scan paper files in your computer and put them in the corresponding family folder for later research, and make sure you upload your digital photos to a desktop computer and/or external hard drive. Make sure you make multiple copies of all important research material—sooner or later, your hard drive will crash, and you don't want to have to repeat your hard work!

Now it's time to start looking at records. Take all of the information you've found and compare it to other sources and the data you've already proven to be true. If a newly discovered name, date, or event at first glance appeared to fit with your research but now doesn't, make a note and return to the fact later. Record-taking inconsistencies or errors, such as spelling variations in names or incorrect or illegible tombstone inscriptions, could help explain a discrepancy.

GRAVE TIP

Say Thank You: Take a few moments before you dig in and send a "thank you" to the folks who helped out. In addition to letting them know you appreciate their time and effort, you'll also help establish a network of locals who can keep you posted on future finds, maybe even paving the way if you ever need a favor.

If you took plenty of photos (You did, right?), go through those as well. Look for symbols or inscriptions you didn't notice in the cemetery, and (if tombstone inscriptions conflict with your previous research) try to look at them in different ways. What else could these symbols mean? Could you have mistaken one letter for another? If stones are difficult to read due to old handwriting, look for a transcribing program that can help you make sense of those notes. Make sure that, like with your cemetery documents, you create multiple back-ups of your photos. See the next section for tips on how to use photo software to digitally enhance your photos.

Once you've analyzed your research, see what holes are in your family's story and whether your new research has helped fill them. What research questions have always plagued you, and can you fill in any information with the materials you've brought back from your trip? Be sure to read and record all parts of a document, as you never know what clues they can hold for a dutiful researcher.

Also be on the lookout for family naming and burial patterns. Pan out and view all your ancestor's information together, perhaps in a five-generation ancestor chart (see appendix A). Names, places, or burial sites that affect multiple ancestors might clue you into another aspect of your family's life, belief system, or traditions. For example, having an ancestor named John in every generation might present a research challenge, but the consistently appearing name tells you that it had a deep connection for your family. Find out why.

Once you've wrapped your head around the research you've already done, start planning your next steps. Identify new lines of research that you've uncovered in your time at the cemetery. Start a file for further research, as one answer may lead to another question—jot down your thoughts as they come to you.

For example, if you discovered from a tombstone that your great-great-grandfather served in the Civil War, investigate those Civil War military records. Which regiment did he serve with? What was his rank? Who was his commander? Did he receive a pension, and (if so) who claimed it? Cemetery research can help answer many genealogy questions, but it raises several new ones as well.

Be especially on the lookout for additional resources you need to consult in future research. If you didn't have a chance to go by the local funeral home for information, for example, get in touch now. Tell funeral home staff what information you're seeking and see if they still have the records—it's amazing what some undertakers kept in their files! Take time to look through old newspapers, as well, to see what family stories you can uncover. Research the time period when your ancestors lived in an area, and do some sleuthing into the region's history to gain a better understanding of what their lives were like.

Once the majority of the paper trail has been dealt with, look for old maps of where your ancestors lived and find the property they owned. With the names and information you gleaned from your cemetery trip (maiden names, in-laws, neighbors, etc.), you may be able to view online property maps by county and find your ancestors' property.

Finally, put all that information in a list. This will be helpful when you plan another trip; all you have to do is print out your latest list of what needs more investigation, and you'll be ready to head out the door.

TOUCHING UP PHOTOS

Once you're home, you may have some cemetery photos whose quality leaves a bit to be desired. You might not have had the appropriate lighting or equipment in the field and so simply took the best picture you could. But you don't have to settle for these low-quality images. Modern technology allows you to manipulate digital photos to make them easier to read. In this section, we'll provide a few tricks and tips to at least perk up (if not salvage) your images so they're readable.

The photo program you use will likely depend on what kind of smartphone/camera and computer you have. I use iPhoto, which offers an edit tab at the bottom of each photo. Let's find out what it can do! (Note: Every photo software program will differ somewhat, but certain key tools are available in all of them. The strategies I outline here should also apply to other photo-editing programs.)

From your desktop computer, open your photo-editing software and import the files you'd like to edit. Alternatively, you can select a file and tell your computer to open it with your photo software. Once you've imported a photo, select it and click the Edit button to view three options: Quick Fixes, Effects, and Adjust. The Quick Fixes button (image **A**) is a simple answer to minor photo problems, with a handful of options:

- **Rotate** can switch the photo from horizontal to vertical and vice versa.
- **Enhance** is the "magic wand" that makes your photos look lighter, brighter and more vivid with just one click. Use this tool to help counter-balance bad lighting.
- **Fix Red-Eye** does just what it says by removing that pesky red-eye flash from the eyes of the people in your photos (though, of

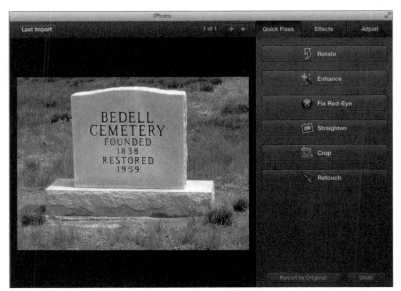

Image A: Photo-editing options under the Quick Fixes tab are good for correcting simple mistakes.

course, most of your images are of monuments and so you won't have this issue).

- **Straighten** is my favorite tool. When shooting in a cemetery, don't expect to come home with perfectly level photos—the ground is never that level. By moving the Straighten slider in the direction you want, you can adjust the photo's orientation. This can help you more easily decipher tombstone writing and symbols.

- The **Crop** tool allows you to trim the photo down to include only what you want to see, as isolating cemetery iconography can sometimes make it easier to understand. I usually make two copies of the photo: the full long shot of the stone or the cemetery, then a cropped close-up view of maybe an epitaph or symbol on a stone.

- **Retouch** is a handy little tool that allows you to erase distractions or imperfections from your photos. Say you shot a gravestone that has bird droppings on the top. With the Retouch tool selected, simply drag your cursor across the top of the stone and it will fill in with the background, removing the unsightly bird mess.

Image B: The Effects tab in iPhoto has more complex tools that will allow you to manipulate the lighting in a photo.

You have more advanced options under the Effects button (image **B**). The six buttons labeled Lighten, Darken, Contrast, Warmer, Cooler, and Saturate allow you to work magic on a photo that might be too dark by applying different filters and adjusting color levels. Make a couple of copies of a photo, then click on the Lighten or Darken button to apply a different brightness level. Likewise, Contrast will heighten the distinctions between light and dark (possibly making text easier to read), and you can manipulate an image's colors to make them "warmer" (bringing out red, brown, and yellow) or cooler (bringing out blue and purple) with the appropriate buttons. The Saturate button makes colors richer, which is probably most useful to you if you'll be displaying your pictures or sharing them with family members.

Other effects are less useful for tombstone tourists, but might still provide entertainment and (in some cases) be useful. For example, you can turn a color photo into black and white/sepia tone, or even give it an antique look. Likewise, the Matte, Vignette, and Edge tabs allow you to create a border around the photo, and the Fade and Boost buttons let you wash out (or heighten) the color. The None button comes in handy when you've overdone the adjustments by setting the photo back to its original tones.

The Adjust menu allows subtle tweaks to photos. Again, start with a couple of copies of the same photo and work with the different slider bars to discover what they do. Once you're familiar with the abilities of each, you can make minute adjustments to photos like the pros.

With your photos cleaned up and organized, now it's time to do some sleuthing.

DIGGING INTO YOUR FAMILY TREE

Let's take a look at cemetery research in action. In the case studies that follow, I'll outline how I used information I found in the cemetery to grow my family tree and enrich my family's story.

Strange Places: Conquering Changing Place-Names

My first foray into family history involved locating my great grandmother, Rachel (Gladish) France's grave. As I described in chapter 1, I found the cemetery with great difficulty, but I had a concrete plan once I knew where I was going—except I hadn't prepared for what I discovered.

According to her death certificate, Rachel France was buried in "Biddel Cemetery" on August 17, 1970. As I later learned, the cemetery was actually named *Bedell* for the Bedell family who occupied a large number of plots. After walking the remote cemetery's perimeter, I found her grave—or should I say *graves?*—in about fifteen minutes. In addition to her grave, I discovered two "bonus" graves: my great-grandfather, Marion France, and his son, Jessie France, someone I had no knowledge of. This was definitely information to tuck away for later research.

Upon returning home, the France mystery intrigued me. Why would the France family (or at least the parents and one child) be buried in the Bedell Family Cemetery? I discovered a Dr. William Bedell of Vincennes who grew up in Johnson Township on a nearby farm owned by his father in the 1850s and '60s. (Could the cemetery be located on part

Image C: Jessie France's death certificate has a curious cause of death: "coronary occlusion."

of that farm? Plat books might yield an answer.) William began studying medicine in 1877 and graduated from the Missouri Medical College in St. Louis three years later. Dr. Bedell lived in Vincennes where he continued to practice medicine. Maybe he had been the France family doctor?

What else could I discover about the France family? I started by researching this "new" relative, Jessie. Thanks to census forms, I knew my great-grandparents lived in Vincennes since the 1920s; indeed, Jessie died there in 1937. In the 1920 and 1930 censuses, Jessie was one of five of their nine children still living at home. According to his death certificate (image **C**), he died of a "coronary occlusion" at the age of eighteen, but someone of his age listed as a "farmer boy" who worked on the farm his whole life was unlikely to die from a heart attack. (Maybe he instead died from a pre-existing heart condition he'd had since birth?) The certificate indicated that Jessie was embalmed and buried in "Biddle" Cemetery on May 2, 1937, with Marion France (his father, my great-grandfather) serving as an informant on the record. The genealogical society didn't have records from the undertaker who created the death certificate, so I was out of luck on that front. I was running out of leads, but I was determined to come up with something.

Little did I expect to find an entire generation of ancestors, least of all while searching for places. Bedell Cemetery was known locally as *Biddle*, located in Johnson Township next to the town of Decker, Indiana (once known as Deckertown). Curious about other place-name changes, I searched for other communities in the area that had changed names and came across a town called White Oak Springs (now Petersburg, Indiana). A historical article from Indiana University explained this was probably the first settlement in the region, providing a list of the town's founding families from 1807 to 1810. As I read, I began to recognize surnames, and I had found several of my ancestors by the time I finished the article. Apparently, my ancestors settled in this "White Oak Springs" after crossing the Ohio River in the early years of the nineteenth century. Rachel France (neé Gladish) was among them, and I now have a long list of her Gladish kin, along with other family names. The article also mentioned a book (*The First Families of White Oak Springs*) that I need to investigate, another item for my to-do list.

Thanks to this find (and to hunches from cemetery research), I discovered more about my ancestors in one afternoon than I ever had before. They lived near the White Oak Springs Fort, keeping vigil against the Indians who threatened their homes and farms. Many times, the entire settlement would go and stay at the fort until the threat of an Indian attack had passed. My seventh great-grandmother was credited with bringing the Cumberland Presbyterian faith across the Ohio River, and my eighth great-grandfather (noted as being Irish) was the only blacksmith in town to own his own tools. What great details!

I have since verified most of the information I found on that day, visiting numerous cemeteries and finding most of the graves of these early Indiana pioneers. I found marriages recorded in church and county records, which helped keep track of how the family grew. Death certificates, likewise, have provided me with essential tidbits from time to time. And those county history books keep offering up clues that need to be investigated.

While I didn't manage to find much more about Jessie France himself, in going to the cemetery, finding his stone, and deciding to dig deeper, I set myself on the path to this once-in-a-decade discovery. What had started as a research exercise for Jessie France had turned into a family reunion, of sorts. The bottom line to cemetery research and genealogy is never be afraid of pursuing a far-fetched idea—you never know where it might lead.

Family Scandals: Separating Fact from Fiction

While researching my maternal fourth great-grandparents (Peter Burkhart and Elizabeth Snyder), I discovered they had died on the same day. Could it have been an accident? Had the couple died of the same disease, hours apart? Digging deeper into this mystery would uncover a family secret of enormous magnitude.

After coming up empty-handed in an online search for death certificates, I traveled to Stewart Cemetery where they were buried. This gave me lots of photos—and a shocking answer to my question. In the cemetery, I could see raw coal pits where mining still occurs, the ragged earth echoing the melancholy of the graveyard. After a few minutes of searching, I found the couple's grave (image **D**) set apart from the

7

Image D: Peter and Elizabeth Burkhart's grave is set apart from others—perhaps to conceal a tragic family secret.

others, a traditional archway used in the 1800s to indicate a married couple. One section of the stone was cracked, but overall it appeared in good shape. When I walked up to it to get close-up shots, I saw the epitaph, which explained why the two died on the same day: "He killed his wife while in a mad rage and then killed himself." This was definitely not what I had expected. I had my answer, but the tale was far from told. I had quite a lot of research still to do.

I wanted to learn more about my ancestor-turned-killer. A stop at the local library netted me a biographical sketch of Peter Burkhart (image **E**) in the History of Pike County, Indiana. According to his biography, Peter was a model citizen who was known as "the greatest hunter and of always keeping the largest number and best bred hounds of any man in the county.... He succeeded well as a farmer." The book went on to describe his family: Elizabeth and Peter married in 1844, and they had nine children. Eight of them had families of their own, all of whom lived nearby.

Biographical sketches of the time present Peter as a wealthy model citizen, well liked by the town: "one of the most successful office holders and prominent pioneer citizens in the county." State census forms backed up Peter's wealth, and plat maps of the time showed him owning a vast amount of land that he had parceled out to his sons over the years.

Everything in the biography also fit what I knew about that branch of my ancestry. My ancestors were pioneers in Indiana, settling in the rich and farmable land of Pike County near what would become the town of Petersburg. Raising dogs for work and companionship had been a part of their lives for generations, and longevity has always been a strong suit—with some members making it just short of one hundred years old. Peter's prominent leadership qualities also fit the narrative. So what had happened for Peter to murder his wife and kill himself?

With no one alive who would know the answer, researching newspapers of the time was my best bet. Sensational news was quite acceptable back then (especially when dealing with such a tragic and scandalous event), so take everything you read with a grain of salt until you can find a way to verify it. With that in mind, I read the Pike County Democrat newspaper and found it to be the least sensational of all of the reports: "The most startling case of [illegible] and suicide which has ever taken place in Pike County. Peter Burkhart shot his wife, Elizabeth with a shotgun. She ran out on the porch, followed by Burkhart, where she soon died. He then took the same gun and emptied it into his heart."

named Edna G.

PETER BURKHART was born in North Carolina, January 26, 1822. His parents, Leonard and Dedida (Smith) Burkhart, were of Dutch and English descent respectively. They were born in Europe and came to North Carolina when quite young. Here they married. They came to Pike County, Ind., about 1835 and passed the remainder of their lives. The father died about 1855 and the mother in 1852. The family came to Indiana when our subject was about thirteen years old. The country at that time was heavily timbered and was inhabited by many wild animals.

[He] killed a deer the first [...] [...]al has always had the reputation [of] being the greatest hunter, [and] of always keeping the largest [n]umber and best bred hounds of any man in the county. He [ki]lled the last deer seen i[n] th[e] county from his house at a dis[tance] of [...] [...] It h[a]s o[n]ly been six years since he captured a large gray wolf about two miles south of his res[id]ence. About seven years ago he had a leg broken while following the hounds and since that time has participated but very little in the chase. He has succeeded well as a farmer and now owns 297½ acres of land having sold 160 acres of his farm. Elizabeth Snyder became his wife April 1, 1844. They became the parents of nine children, eight of whom are married and living within three miles of their father. They all have families but none of their children have died. The family history presents remarkable instances of longevity. He has always been a Democrat in politics and has served as township trustee six terms. During his first term the township was in debt over $100, but he soon paid the debt, and during war times it had a debt of over $3,000. In two years this was paid off and the township is in a flourishing condition. His last two terms he brought the township out with a cash balance of about $1,500. He has been urged by his many friends to run for higher offices but he has invariably declined. He has been one of the most successful office holders and prominent pioneer citizens of the county.

Image E: A biographical sketch of Peter Burkhart paints him as a model citizen. So what led him to murder?

Wow! That was stunning to see in print. From there, I began to check other local papers, then branched out to regional reports.

Since it was horrifying and dramatic, the story was carried throughout southern Indiana. One paper reported that a local boy heard the shots and summoned neighbors. Another local newspaper headline read "An Awful Tragedy .. Frenzied by Jealousy, an Old Man Slaughters His Wife and Then Kills Himself" (image **F**).

Apparently, tales became more lurid as they left the immediate community that had known the Burkharts, and I had to take extra care to parse out the fact from the fiction. A regional paper, the *Vincennes Weekly Western Sun*, slanted the information a different way with the headline, "Monster at Work in Pike County ... An Old Husband Murders His Young Wife and Then Suicides" (image **G**). "*Young*" wife? Peter was born January 26, 1822, and Elizabeth was born two years later on October 11, 1824. Elizabeth was sixty-three years old at the time of her murder! So much for the "jealous of the young wife" angle.

Regardless of the location, newspapers all stated Peter's motive was jealousy. One notes him as "crazed of the 'green-eyed monster'... accus[ing] his aged and faithful wife of marriage infidelity," while another states "He was not too old to be jealous of the young wife, whom he had married late in life...whether she gave her aged husband any real cause for jealously does not appear."

Yet another paper mentions that "he was given to drinking whisky and when under the influence was very jealous of his wife..." And another newspaper article ends with the line, "It is thought he was insane."

The *Vincennes Weekly Western Sun* provided another interesting detail: Peter's will (image **H**). The paper claimed his five daughters had been denied his estate because their husbands were "the bane of old Burkhart's suspicion—of intimacy with their aged mother-in-law." Another paper told the same story: Peter "hated his son-in-laws [sic] and charged them with undue intimacy with his aged wife."

Seeing allegations like this, I knew I had to see Peter's will myself to get some answers. After some research, I found four handwritten pages. Peter left his "beloved wife Elizabeth" the bulk of his acreage and estate at the time the will was made, two years before the murder.

Image F: You can often learn about your ancestors' more salacious stories in contemporary newspapers.

AN AWFUL TRAGEDY.

Particulars of the Pike County Horror.

Frenzied by Jealousy. an Old Man Slaughters His Wife and Then Kills Himself.

JEALOUSY.

The Monster at Work in Pike County,

And an Old Husband Murders His Young Wife and Then Suicides.

Image G: Some publications sensationalized the Burkhart story more than others.

But if Peter questioned her fidelity, would he have left hundreds of acres of valuable farmland to a woman he did not trust? It seemed an odd question to have to consider, but relevant given the circumstances. However, the will seemed to support another of the newspaper's claim. Only four of his nine children were mentioned: sons Noah Ark, Adam Gideon, and General Burkhart, and one daughter, Caroline (Burkhart) Morgan. Peter closed his will by writing, "The remainder I authorize to be sold off at public auction and the proceeds of the sale be used to pay my personal debts."

The will was silent on Peter's reasoning, but the press went on to say, "There is a feeling that only one thing can be done ... and that is by breaking the will of the deceased so that all of his children will share alike in his property." Peter had three men witness his written will and signature, evidently adamant that five of the girls were not to inherit anything from his estate. Regardless of what this feud was really about, he was making sure his five daughters were punished.

Did Peter Burkhart act out of jealously on that fateful July night in 1887? No one knows for sure, but I intend to keep digging to find out what can help me understand it. And who knows what other family secrets I may uncover.

The family had many reasons for letting this secret pass quickly and quietly into history. But unfortunately, with my direct-line ancestors

BURKHART'S WILL.

The Decree of the Pike County Wife Murderer and Suicide in the Courts.

A most sensational case of will-breaking is to be tried in the Pike Circuit Court, and the facts that leak out are most too monstrous for belief. A few days ago Peter Burkhart killed his wife, by emptying his shot-gun in her body, and then turned the gun on himself and suicided. Burkhart was 65 years old and his wife was 63. He was insanely jealous of his gray-haired spouse and made life a hell on earth to her. Burkhardt left property to the amount of twenty-five thousand dollars. He was the father of nine children. Six were married, and he hated his six sons-in-law. Even more than that he charged them all with undue

Image H: This article about Burkhart's will lends support to the theory that he hated five of his daughters and so wrote them out of his will.

(including my grandparents, who may have known parts of the real story) gone, I'm on my own. Even in this day and age, some will want to "protect the family secret" of a murder-suicide that happened more than one hundred years ago. But this is what genealogy is all about: researching and discovering facts about your ancestors, including the life celebrations, hardships, and unexplained decisions they made.

KEYS from the CRYPT

• Analyze your cemetery research finds and compare them to the work you've already done. Look for any discrepancies, and figure out what may have caused them.

• Make a list of what other research you need to do and what resources you'll need to consult.

• Use photo-editing software such as iPhoto to make your images easier to read.

Recording Cemetery Data Online

N ow that you're back from the cemetery and have worked the information you found there into your research, what can you do? Like other genealogical data, the best way to utilize and preserve your cemetery research is to put it online. Cemetery research is particularly important to enter into online databases, as other researchers may be longing to find the same tombstone or death certificate that you've uncovered during your trip to the cemetery.

With so many genealogy websites available, it's difficult to decide where to spend your time. In this chapter, we'll discuss the four websites that are most useful for tombstone tourists.

BILLIONGRAVES

As we discussed in chapter 3, BillionGraves <**www.billiongraves.com**> is the world's largest free directory of searchable GPS cemetery information, and uploading your data to this site can help others locate the resources you've been researching—and help you pinpoint your ancestor's grave should you ever need to find it again.

Taking and Uploading Gravestone Photos

With the free BillionGraves mobile app, you can take photos at any cemetery on your smartphone or tablet. (Note: You must use a smartphone to take and upload the photos in order to apply the GPS locations.) Here's how:

STEP 1 Set up your device. Download the BillionGraves app onto your smartphone, then log in to your account. If you haven't set up a BillionGraves account, see the instructions in chapter 3.

STEP 2 Photograph the tombstone. At the cemetery, hit the Take Pictures button to open the camera. As you'll see, the app uses your location to place you in a cemetery. Remember to keep your feet out of the picture, and make sure your shadow is not in the photo. (We're going for nice clean images!)

1

2

3

4

STEP 3 Review your photo. Review your picture, and select the option Retake to delete the current picture and take another shot, then click Use to upload the photo and Don't Ask Again to disable the review for future photos.

STEP 4 Upload the photo. Once you click Use, the photo (along with its geographic information) will be uploaded to the BillionGraves database. The image will be transcribed by BillionGraves' army of volunteers (see the next section).

Transcribing Photos

While you're taking inventory of the tombstones you want and uploading them to the BillionGraves database, why not take the time to transcribe them (and maybe some other photos), too? BillionGraves allows you to provide written accounts of what appears on a tombstone, offering a host of tools that help you digitally record what appears in a tombstone image. Here's how to transcribe a photo; visit "Transcription Help" for tips and suggestions <billiongraves.com/how-to-transcribe>:

Volunteering with BillionGraves

Interested in becoming involved with the BillionGraves community? The database functions as more than a database of tombstone records—users can also request photos of cemetery markers. People from all over the world photograph gravestones and submit them to BillionGraves.

As a result, BillionGraves volunteers are the lifeblood of the organization. You don't need special setup, equipment, training, or paperwork to become a volunteer. All you need is a smartphone and the BillionGraves app, which allow you to take GPS-encoded photos of grave markers in cemeteries all over the world. When you're finished, upload the pictures to BillionGraves for transcription. Once transcribed, the cemetery markers are made available to the public for family history research.

The site estimates that one volunteer can record more than five hundred images in one hour, making it a great way for you and your family members or fellow cemetery buffs to spend a day. Check the maps on BillionGraves to find local cemeteries needing to be photographed or with outstanding photo requests, then map them out and spend the day shooting.

Cemetery shooting, particularly for volunteer work, is a fantastic activity for business or community projects. Everyone can participate in the planning details, and the activity builds teamwork skills while accomplishing a much-needed service. Check out **<www.billiongraves.com/service>** for more information and a packet of tips for groups. If you'd like to help but don't want to be in charge of the arrangements, e-mail BillionGraves at *support@billiongraves.com*, and its team will help coordinate a group in your area.

Want to stay away from the camera? You can also help the BillionGraves community by transcribing images other users have taken.

STEP **1** **Find a photo.** Go to the BillionGraves Transcription page <www.billiongraves.com/transcribe>. You'll be automatically presented with a photo that another user has uploaded but still needs transcription.

STEP **2** **Select a language.** At the top of the page, you can select a Headstone Language from the dropdown menu that indicates what language the text is in. Click OK to confirm. If the photo depicts a headstone that's in a language you can't read (or you want to move on to a different tombstone), click the blue Skip button in the top right.

STEP **3** **Rate the photo.** BillionGraves requires transcriptions to include a rating, which helps the site categorize photos and filter out inappropriate or irrelevant images. In the bottom right-hand corner, click the red Rate Image button to select from a variety of options,

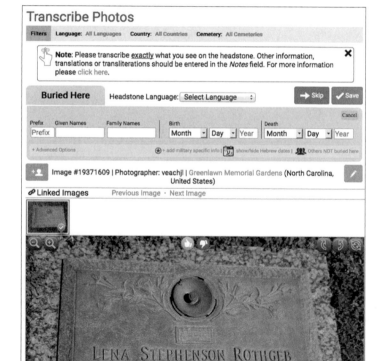

including Good photo/headstone, Bad photo (unreadable), Bad headstone (unreadable), and No information to transcribe. Select the appropriate response, then click Save and OK to confirm.

STEP 4 Input transcriptions. Use the fields at the top of the page to enter all legible names and dates exactly as they appear on the tombstone. Click the Advanced Options link to add an additional

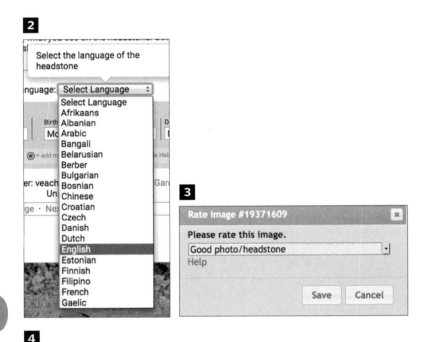

5

Buried Here — Greenlawn Memorial Gardens (North Carolina, United States)

→ Next

Lena Rothgeb (Stephenson) — Born: 24 Apr 1937 — Died: 1 Dec 1975 — Married: Not Available

edit | FamilySearch

Others NOT Buried Here: — hide

Given Names: | Family Names: | *Relationship: Relationship | + Add

Grave Epitaph — edit

Grave Information

* Some transcription information may be from linked images

Linked Images — Previous Image · Next Image

line with maiden name, marriage information, suffix, and age at death. You can also toggle military-specific info by clicking the link next to the star within a circle, or add information about individuals not buried in the grave by clicking Others NOT buried here. When you're finished, click the green Save button.

STEP 5 Review your transcription. The page will update to include a listing of the information you've transcribed, and any unfilled fields will remain. In addition, you can add information to two new fields (Grave Epitaph, for any other text appearing on the headstone, and Grave Information, for any notes about symbols, markings, or other noteworthy details). Fill these in if necessary and click Save to finalize your edits. If you want to edit your transcription, click the blue edit button, make your changes, and click the Save button to finalize. When you're finished, click the green Next button; the photo and its transcription will be available from the BillionGraves search page.

8

FIND A GRAVE

As we discussed in chapter 3, Find A Grave <www.findagrave.com> touts more than 159 million burial records and 75 million photos. The entries on the site (called "memorials") also include obituary and biographical information, plus personal memories from those who knew the deceased.

Creating a Memorial

Creating an ancestor's memorial allows you to record your information and share it with others while also serving as a tribute to your ancestor and a place for mourning and remembrance for you and other loved ones. Best of all, it's quick and easy (and free)! Here's how to create a memorial page for your ancestor:

STEP **1** **Create an account/log in.** You don't need an account on Find A Grave to search for memorials and burial records, but you will need to register to add or edit memorials. See chapter 3 for instructions on setting up an account.

STEP **2** **Search for your ancestor.** No sense in creating a memorial if one already exists! Fill in the search form with your ancestor's information and try to find him in the database to make sure the memo-

FIND A GRAVE

A Grave Interest | Sign out

Billy Wilder died on this date 15 years ago.

Find Famous Graves

See the graves of thousands of famous people from around the world.

- Famous Grave Search
- Browse by **Location**
- Browse by **Claim to Fame**
- Search by **Date**
  - Born On This Date
  - Died On This Date
- **Most Popular** Searches
- Yearly Necrologies
- Posthumous Reunions
- Interesting Monuments
- Interesting Epitaphs

Find Graves

Find the graves of ancestors, create virtual memorials, add 'virtual flowers' and a note to a loved one's grave, etc.

- Search **159 million** grave records
- Search for a cemetery
- Add burial records
- View recently added names
- Stroll through our online cemetery
- Join the Find A Grave Community
- Top 50 Contributors
- Link To Find A Grave
- Surname index

2

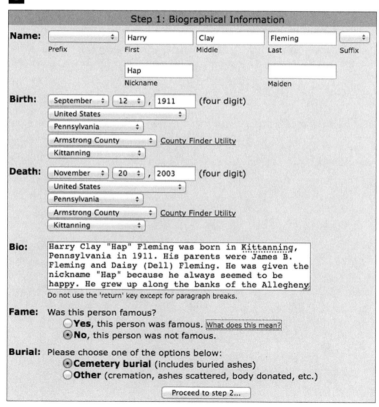

Find A Grave Search Form

Name: | Harry | | | | Fleming |
First | Middle | Last (required)

Include maiden name(s) in my search ☐
Do partial name search on surname ☐

Born: In ⬍ **Year:** 1911

Died: In ⬍ **Year:** 2003

Cemetery in: – Country List – ⬍
– US State List – ⬍

Memorial #:

Date filter: All Names ⬍

Order by: Name ⬍

Search

3

Step 1: Biographical Information

Name: [⬍] | Harry | Clay | Fleming | [⬍]
Prefix | First | Middle | Last | Suffix

Hap
Nickname | Maiden

Birth: September ⬍ 12 ⬍ , 1911 (four digit)
United States ⬍
Pennsylvania ⬍
Armstrong County ⬍ County Finder Utility
Kittanning ⬍

Death: November ⬍ 20 ⬍ , 2003 (four digit)
United States ⬍
Pennsylvania ⬍
Armstrong County ⬍ County Finder Utility
Kittanning ⬍

Bio: Harry Clay "Hap" Fleming was born in Kittanning, Pennsylvania in 1911. His parents were James B. Fleming and Daisy (Dell) Fleming. He was given the nickname "Hap" because he always seemed to be happy. He grew up along the banks of the Allegheny
Do not use the 'return' key except for paragraph breaks.

Fame: Was this person famous?
○ **Yes**, this person was famous. What does this mean?
⦿ **No**, this person was not famous.

Burial: Please choose one of the options below:
⦿ **Cemetery burial** (includes buried ashes)
○ **Other** (cremation, ashes scattered, body donated, etc.)

Proceed to step 2...

8

rial you want to create does not already exist. (See chapter 3 for more detailed instructions on searching for your ancestors on Find A Grave.) If you find your ancestor, you can view the information, add/edit details or photos, and leave virtual flowers. I'm looking for information about my ancestor, Harry Fleming, but he doesn't yet have a page. I'll have to make one for him.

STEP 3 Input biographical information. If you can't find your ancestor's pre-existing memorial, fill out the biographical information form at <www.findagrave.com/cgi-bin/fg.cgi?page=ds> (also accessible by clicking Add Burial Records under the Actions column on the left side of the page, then clicking Family and Friends). You'll be asked for your ancestor's name (first, middle, last, and maiden, plus any nicknames), birth year and place, death year and place, and a short bio that describes the deceased's life. You'll also be asked whether the person was famous (i.e., whether she should be included in the website's database of famous people), which the site defines as a notable public figure. Finally, you can indicate whether the burial was in a cemetery or "other." When you're finished, click Proceed to step 2.

STEP 4 Add a cemetery. Input the name of the cemetery where your ancestor is buried, as well as the cemetery's country, state, and county. Find A Grave will search for a cemetery already in its database. Review the results (and view a map if necessary), then add a

8

GRAVE TIP

Mind Your Permissions: Don't worry about other users editing your beloved ancestor's page—as the page's owner, you are the only one who can edit the page's details. If you'd like to forfeit this responsibility (or if you've created a memorial for another user's ancestor and want to give them access), you can permanently transfer ownership of the memorial to another Find A Grave user by clicking the Transfer Management on the memorial page.

4

Step 2: Find The Cemetery - Harry Fleming

Please enter the first few letters of the cemetery Harry Fleming is buried in and then click the 'Search for the cemetery' button. If the cemetery is in the United States, you must also choose a state.

Cemetery Name:
Do not use abbreviations
Why can't I enter the full cemetery name?

Country: The United States

State: – US State List –

Search for the cemetery

plot number if you know it. Click Add this Name to finish, and you'll be taken to a page that confirms your memorial was set up and gives you links to view it or to add more names from the same or a different cemetery.

STEP **5** **Review your memorial and edit information.** You can review the memorials you've created at any time by going to your account page (click your username under "Logged in as" in the Actions column on the website's left side) or by finding your ancestor using the search form or the memorial's unique ID number. From the memorial page, you can edit individual sections of the memorial or add additional features (such as photos), by clicking the appropriate fields. Notably, you can upload photos of either the person or his tombstone. Once completed, the memorial will look something like this.

Find A Grave Changes

8

As of this book's publication, Find A Grave was still developing a new, more modern look for its site. The beta version showcased a few noticeable changes, including a prominent search box on the home page, simpler search options, revised memorial pages, and more integration with the Find A Grave mobile app. While Find A Grave might look different in this book than it does on your screen, the underlying mechanics and functionality of the site are the same.

Harry Clay "Hap" Fleming [Edit Name]

| Memorial | Photos | Flowers | | Share | Edit |

Learn about upgrading this memorial...

[Transfer Management] [Edit] [Delete]

Birth: Sep. 12, 1911
Kittanning
Armstrong County
Pennsylvania, USA
Death: Nov. 20, 2003
Kittanning
Armstrong County
Pennsylvania, USA [Edit Dates]

Added by: A Grave Interest

Harry Clay "Hap" Fleming was born in Kittanning, Pennsylvania in 1911. His parents were James B. Fleming and Daisy (Dell) Fleming. He was given the nickname "Hap" because he always seemed to be happy. He grew up along the banks of the Allegheny River and spent many childhood weekends playing with Jimmy Stewart (later, a well-known American actor).

Added by: Felicia (Foltz) Hoffman

Hap was a Big Band piano player in the 1930's and 40's. He met his wife, Annis Skaggs while both were performing on the road. They married August 28, 1950 and settled in Robinson, Illinois where Annis was from. Hap and Annis were good friends with author and local Robinson boy, James Jones (From Here to Eternity; Some Came Running). Hap worked in insurance industry for several years. He continued to play in bands until the 1960's and was a lifelong artist. Hap was president and volunteered at the Crawford County Historical Society for years.

Hap moved back to his hometown of Kittanning, PA after Annis died in 1992. He died there in 2003 after a lengthy illness. He was preceded in death by his parents, an infant brother, his wife Annis, one sister, Romaine I Laird, and one brother, Cecil Vernon Fleming. His brother Jack Fleming survived him by two weeks.

Cemetery Photo
Don't show cemetery photos
on this memorial [?]
Added by: Robert Stephenson

Hap was cremated and his remains were buried beside his wife's at the Oblong Cemetery in Oblong, Illinois.

Learn more about Hap @
http://agraveinterest.blogspot.com/2011/11
/remembering-life-well-lived-harry-hap.html
[Edit Bio]

 Add a photo for this person Request A Photo

Change Photo Order

Photos may be scaled.
Click on image for full size.

With the Find A Grave app (which is available for both iOS and Android devices), you can upload multiple headstones at once from the field—though, unlike the BillionGraves app, it won't automatically preserve your upload location.

STEP 1 Find your memorial or cemetery. Unlike the BillionGraves app, the Find A Grave app requires you to find a specific memorial or cemetery to add photos to. Follow the steps in chapter 3 to find the memorial or cemetery on the app you want to contribute to; click the camera in the upper-right corner of a memorial's page to add photos, and click Add Headstone Photos on a cemetery's page. In this example, I added photos to the Carpenter's Run Pioneer Cemetery in Blue Ash, Ohio.

STEP 2 Take and upload your photo(s). You have the option of either taking a photo through the Find A Grave app or uploading an image from your phone's album that you've already taken. You can review all the photos you've uploaded on your profile page.

STEP 3 Transcribe your photo(s). Type the tombstone's information in the appropriate fields, filling in whatever you can read. Photos you haven't transcribed after seven days will be open to the public.

STEP 4 Match the photo with a memorial. The Find A Grave app will search for memorials whose details match the transcription you've provided. Select the appropriate memorial, or follow the prompts to create a new memorial if none has been created.

8

USGENWEB

While not focusing exclusively on cemeteries or death records, USGen-Web (USGW) is still a valuable resource for tombstone tourists and genealogists alike. Run by a large group of volunteers, USGW began in 1996 to provide free genealogy access to everyone and is made up of individual sites that represent every state and county in the United States. Today, USGW has thousands of sites containing millions of pages of genealogical and historical information, plus several special projects pages including the Tombstone Transcription Project.

The Family Tree Cemetery Field Guide

Because more than two thousand volunteers oversee the individual pages that make up USGW, each site is organized differently, and different sites have different resources. Besides general family history records and transcriptions provided by volunteers, you may also find news of scheduled family reunions, state histories, online genealogy books, research tips, scanned family pedigrees, maps, and even lost photos and orphaned Bibles. But all USGW sites have at least one thing in common: All the data is available for free.

From the homepage <**www.usgenweb.org**>, select the state you're researching in (image **A**). The information on the consortium of websites is organized by state, then (usually) by county. I'm researching ancestors from my home state of Indiana, so I clicked the Hoosier State from the interactive map.

Each state site will look different. Image **B** shows INGenWeb, Indiana's USGW affiliate. Here, you'll find links to Indiana information: what's new in the ninety-two counties, historical links, military and orphan train records, and RootsWeb sources. You can also find information on becoming an INGenWeb volunteer.

In addition to viewing information on individual states, you can also participate in one of several projects hosted by USGW that benefit the genealogical community. The one most relevant to this guide is the USGW Tombstone Transcription Project; you can learn about the others in the Special Projects sidebar.

The Tombstone Transcription Project

The Tombstone Transcription Project <**www.usgwtombstones.org/index.html**> began as a way of getting people to cemeteries to transcribe information carved on grave markers.

Because the United States contains so many cemeteries, this project is always in need of volunteers—and becoming a volunteer is easy. Contact your state's tombstone project manager (see <**www.usgwtombstones.org/registry.html**> for a list) to express an interest. Make sure you provide the name of the cemetery you want to research (plus the county where it is located), along with the name or names of

Image A: The volunteer-run USGenWeb hosts several genealogy projects and has a network of state affiliates.

Image B: Individual state websites can link you to local resources.

the people doing the transcribing. Enter *Tombstone Transcription Project* in the e-mail subject line of the message.

Once you've heard back from the state tombstone project volunteer, find out what entity has legal jurisdiction over the cemetery you will be visiting, and get permission to record the stones. For a public cemetery, contact the sexton or superintendent's office. Also check to see if the office has a plat map of the cemetery and copies of burial records. If the cemetery is abandoned, find out who owns the land and gain their permission to be on the property. Next, check with your local library, genealogical society or archives to establish if any transcription work has been already been completed.

Special Projects

In addition to hosting various state websites and providing research resources for genealogists, USGW organizes a number of projects that serve slightly different purposes for the genealogical community, including:

- The USGenWeb African American Griots Project: This is a central depository for African American records.
- The USGenWeb Archives Project: Materials submitted include transcriptions of birth, marriage, and death records along with wills, probate records, bibles, newspapers, military records, and biographies.
- The USGenWeb Genealogical Events Project: This contains listings of family history events taking place in the United States.
- The USGenWeb Kidz Project: This project helps kids learn about genealogy and how to begin a search.
- The USGenWeb Lineage Project: This project provides a list of others searching for the same descendant.
- The USGenWeb Tombstone Transcription Project: The Tombstone Transcription Project is one of the best-known special projects that USGenWeb sponsors. Volunteers assist by going to cemeteries and transcribing gravestone information. This chapter discusses this project in detail.

Visit <**www.usgenweb.org/about/projects.html**> to learn more about these and other USGW projects.

8

Image C: Accurately recording tombstone information is important for researchers, especially those helping with transcription projects.

If you already have gravestone transcriptions, you can send them to USGW directly so the information becomes accessible to family historians around the world.

Once you're in the graveyard, be sure to record all of the information on the tombstone. Do not change the spelling or punctuation—write it down exactly as it appears. You should also take a photo of each stone in order to keep a visual record of the information.

For example, in transcribing the grave marker for Columbus and Salena Gladish (image **C**), you would note:

Last Name	First Name	Birth	Death
Gladish	Columbus	1845	1917
Gladish	Salena	1848	1933
Stone decorated with lily and fleur-de-lis			

No doubt there is a story here that someone will delve deeper into, and hopefully share their findings with USGW.

When you have completed recording information from the cemetery, submit your transcriptions to the tombstone project manager for the correct state.

8

The USGenWeb Archives Project, one of the site's special projects, has sub-project categories that may also interest you. Some include the Archives Census Images Project (which digitizes images of US census records), the Archives Digital Map Project (high-quality archival and research maps), and the Pension Project (which accepts transcriptions of pensions prior to 1900); see **<www.usgenweb.org/about/projects. html>** for a full list.

But perhaps most interesting is the Obituaries Project, which contains published obituaries archived from newspapers for research. This project began in 2000 when newspapers around the country granted permission to USGW to archive published obituaries. Some obituaries are already in the public domain, while obituaries considered current—those created after 1949—might be extracts or abstracts.

Finding Obituaries on USGenWeb

An obituary can provide us with so much information, especially if someone close to the family wrote it. During the late nineteenth and early twentieth century, these notices became mini biographies about the deceased, with a wealth of details included. Here are suggestions on how to locate that elusive obituary using USGW:

- Start with the Obituaries Project records and search the state and county where the death occurred and would have been published. Also check adjoining counties to see if the announcement was carried in other newspapers.
- Visit the USGW Archives state and county page where the death occurred and search obituaries.
- Post a query on the RootsWeb Message Board in the correct state and county.
- Contact USGW to locate a look-up volunteer who might be able to help.
- Check with other groups that may have access to the obituaries, including the newspaper that published it (if still in business), the local funeral home that handled the arrangements, and local organizations (libraries, historical societies, genealogical organizations, and Family History Centers).

8

Volunteers are always looking for new records, so you have several opportunities to get involved. Here are a few:

- Contact your local and regional papers to gain permission for USGW to archive their published obituaries or determine if its archive contains old obituaries that could be transcribed.
- Catalog your newspaper's obituaries for easier research.
- Visit your local genealogical society and search for pre-1929 obituaries on microfilm to transcribe.

■ HARRY C. FLEMING
⊘ Obituary

Harry C. "Hap" Fleming, 92, 223 East Brady Road, Kittanning, formerly of Robinson, Ill., died Thursday, Nov. 20, 2003 at the Armstrong County Health Center, Kittanning, after several months of declining health.

He was born Sept. 12, 1911 in Kittanning to James Boyd and Daisy (Dell) Fleming. Mr. Fleming was a retired real estate associate with McKamy Realty, Robinson, Ill., curator for the Crawford County Historical Museum for many years and was a radio disc jockey on WTAY Radio. An Army veteran, he served during World War II. His memberships included the Crawford County Genealogical Society, Sons of the American Revolution, Crawford County Council for the Arts and James Jones Preservation Society. Survivors include one brother, Jack M. Fleming of Austin, Minn.; one sister-in-law, Sylvia Skaggs of Stoy, Ill.; and nieces and nephews. He was preceded in death by his parents; his wife, Annis E. (Skaggs) Fleming, whom he married Aug. 28, 1950 and who died Jan. 23, 1992; three brothers, C. Vernon Fleming, James B. Fleming and infant Arthur Fleming; and two sisters, Romaine Laird and Anne C. Stivanson.

FLEMING -- Friends of Harry C. "Hap" Fleming, 92, 223 East Brady Road, Kittanning, formerly of Robinson, Ill., who died Nov. 20, 2003, will be received from 5 p.m. until a Twilight Memorial Service at 7 p.m. Dec. 19 at the Pulliam Funeral Home, Robinson, Ill. with the Rev. Esther Pfeiffer officiating. Burial will be in Oblong Cemetery, Oblong, Ill. Memorials may be made to the James Jones Society or the Crawford County Courthouse Restoration. Arrangements by Pulliam.

Published in Leader Times on Dec. 6, 2003

Image D: Extracting obituaries will allow you to standardize the information you find in them.

8

- Take a trip to the state archives and transcribe obits in the public domain.
- Transcribe obituaries from newspapers that have already granted permission.

When transcribing an obituary, most of the information requested deals with the deceased and his family. Harry C. Fleming's obituary is shown in image **D**, and its transcription/extraction would look like this:

Name	Harry C. "Hap" Fleming
Age	92
City/County/ State of Residence	Kittanning, Pennsylvania (formerly of Robinson, Ill.)
Death/Place	Nov. 20, 2003 at Armstrong County Health Center, Kittanning, Pennsylvania
Birth/Place	Sept. 12, 1911 in Kittanning
Father	James Boyd Fleming
Mother	Daisy (Dell) Fleming
Spouse(s)	Annis E. (Skaggs) Fleming (m. Aug. 28, 1950, d. Jan. 23, 1992)
Son(s)	
Daughter(s)	
Sister(s)	Romaine Laird (deceased,) Anne C. Stivanson (deceased)
Brother(s)	C. Vernon Fleming (deceased), James B. Fleming (deceased), Arthur Fleming (deceased), Jack M. Fleming
Grandchildren	
Funeral Home	Pulliam Funeral Home, Robinson, Ill
Burial Location	Oblong Cemetery, Oblong, Ill
Other Information	• Died after several months of declining health • Retired real estate associate for McKamy Realty, Robinson, Ill • Curator for Crawford County Historical Museum • Radio disc jockey on WTAY Radio • Army veteran, served in World War II • Membership in Crawford County Genealogical Society; Sons of the American Revolution; Crawford County Council for the Arts; James Jones Preservation Society
Extract Source	Leader Times, published Dec. 6, 2003

8

FAMILYSEARCH

FamilySearch is the largest genealogy organization in the world, and all of its resources are free. Organized by the Church of Jesus Christ of Latter-day Saints, the organization was founded in 1894 as the Genealogical Society of Utah (GSU) and began microfilming records in 1938. Over the decades, the group has acquired hundreds of millions of records, storing them in its Family History Library in Salt Lake City and across its more than four thousand branch libraries (now called Family History Centers).

FamilySearch <www.familysearch.org> hit the Internet in November 2005, opening up those decades of research for genealogists around the world. Since then, FamilySearch has announced partnerships with Ancestry.com, BillionGraves, FindMyPast, and MyHeritage, increasing the number of records and sharing capabilities of all the organizations. And even if you can't find a set of records online (or if you'd prefer to view original records), you can have books or microfilm reels delivered to your local Family History Center for in-person inspection—all for free.

In short: FamilySearch is the mother lode of genealogy records, perfect for those who want to do their genealogy without paying a lot of money. All you need to get started is a free account.

The *Unofficial Guide to FamilySearch.org* by Dana McCullough (Family Tree Books, 2015) covers how to use the site in detail, but this section will quickly outline the major search functions on FamilySearch.org.

To begin, log in or create an account at FamilySearch <**www. familysearch.org**>. Having a free account allows you to save records that you come across, build online family trees, and attach records to your ancestor's profile.

Your first stop will likely be the Historical Records search form <**www.familysearch.org/search**> (image **E**), where you can conduct a search of the site's billions of records using your ancestor's name, birth/ marriage/death information, and more. This will search two separate databases—one for records, and the other for family trees. If you'd like to more specifically target your search, you can use the Research by

Location map or the Find a Collection field to find specific record collections to search.

If you'd prefer to find already published family trees, you can also search the Genealogies tab <**www.familysearch.org/family-trees**> (image **F**) to see if there are any family trees that relate to yours. Remember that accuracy of the information on each tree varies, and you should always check what you find against other sources.

Want to go offline? Search using the Catalog link <**www.familysearch. org/catalog/search**> (image **G**) by surname, place, titles, author, subjects, or keywords. This search will turn up all genealogical materials held by FamilySearch, not just those that have been digitized and made available online. You can then request individual microfilm reels, including city and county directories, court records, land and property deeds, maps, military records, slavery and bondage indexes, vital records, and public records.

Image E: You'll likely spend most of your research time on FamilySearch.org using the main Search form.

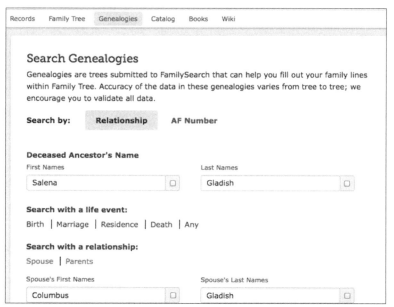

Image F: Search Genealogies to find your ancestors in already published family trees.

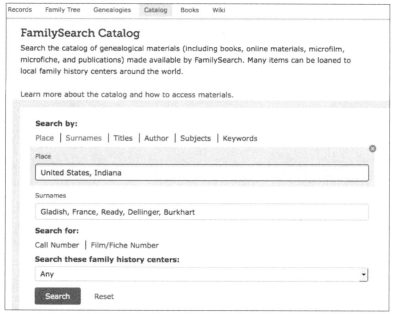

Image G: The FamilySearch Catalog will help you find both offline and online resources held by the Church of Jesus Christ of Latter-day Saints.

Finally, the Books tab connects you to a collection of more than 325,000 digitized publications that pertain to family history and genealogy.

For more in-depth explanations and answers to frequently asked questions, visit the FamilySearch Blog <**www.familysearch.org/blog/en**> and search *How to use FamilySearch.*

Adding and Editing Information to an Ancestor Profile

One of FamilySearch's most famous (and useful) tools is its worldwide, online Family Tree. Here, you can maintain a profile for your deceased ancestors that contains his picture and vital information, plus any records and memories you have. You can even attach records that you find elsewhere on the site to your ancestors' profiles, making research easy. Here's how you can add and edit an ancestor's profile:

STEP 1 **Add your ancestor's profile to your family tree (if necessary).** If the person whose information you add isn't currently on your family tree, you'll need to add her to your branch using other relatives. (If your ancestor is already in your family tree, skip to step 3.) Go to your branch of FamilySearch's Family Tree by clicking Family Tree from the main menu toolbar. Navigate to a parent or child of the person whose information you'd like to upload, then click Add Husband/Wife (if your researched ancestor is the father or mother of someone in your tree) or, from a couple's Children

8

GRAVE TIP

Protect Privacy: When working with online family trees, keep in mind that information you share on the Web can be seen by others. Some sites, such as Ancestry.com <**www.ancestry.com**>, will allow you to keep your tree private, but FamilySearch.org makes profiles for all deceased ancestors public. Note that profiles of people listed as living are kept private in most family trees, including Ancestry.com and FamilySearch.

1

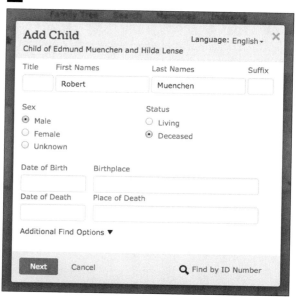

2

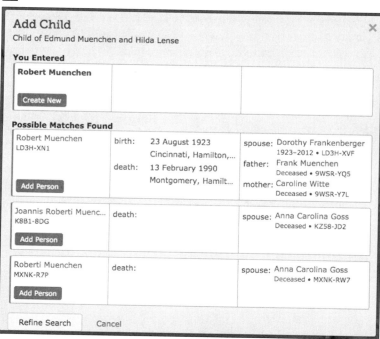

3

Christening
➕ Add

Death
12 July 1960
Logan, Ohio, United States

Modified | History
25 September 2015 by kocha1

Sources | Tag ❶

🌿 Edmund Muenchen, "United States Social Security Death Index"

Burial
➕ Add

dropdown menu, Add Child (if your researched ancestor is the child of someone in your tree). You'll be prompted to enter the person's name and any birth/death information.

STEP 2 View your results. Unlike other online family trees, the Family Tree on FamilySearch.org hopes to one day be one, single family tree for all of humanity—with each historical person having just one profile in its database. As a result, this "one tree" model discourages people from creating duplicate profiles, and you'll need to search for pre-existing ancestor profiles before you can add someone to your tree. Evaluate your search results to see if another user has already created a profile for your ancestor. If you feel confident that your ancestor's profile hasn't been created, click Create New to make a new profile, or Add Person to attach the existing profile to your family tree.

STEP 3 Edit information. When viewing your family tree, click a person's name to see a pop-up that displays his basic information. Click the name to view the full profile, where you can edit a whole host of information. Cemetery researchers will likely want to edit birth, death, and burial dates, which you can access under Vital

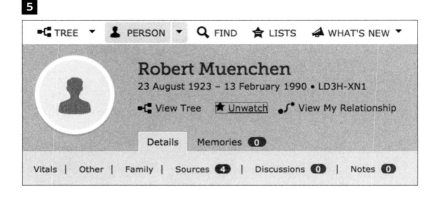

4

▼ Sources

Source Title (Required)

Example: England, Death Certificate of Hugh S. Smith - (1832-1912)

Web Page (Link to the Record)

⊙ WEB PAGE URL   ○ ADD A MEMORY

Example: http://www.uk1841census.com/census_online.htm

Where the Record Is Found (Citation)

Example: UK Census, 1841, Arbroath, Perth, Scotland. Population schedule. Dwelling address. Fed

5

◄ TREE ▼   👤 PERSON ▼   🔍 FIND   ★ LISTS   📣 WHAT'S NEW ▼

Robert Muenchen
23 August 1923 – 13 February 1990 • LD3H-XN1

◄ View Tree   ★ Unwatch   ⌁ View My Relationship

Details   Memories **0**

Vitals | Other | Family | Sources **4** | Discussions **0** | Notes **0**

Information. To add or edit a vital date, click Add under the appropriate heading, or click the information already there, then edit. FamilySearch lets you add notes about your reasoning, which you can add in the Reason This Information Is Correct field. Make sure you hit the Save button to preserve your changes!

STEP 4 Add sources. Always cite your sources! Scroll to the Sources section on your ancestor's profile, where you'll see a list of records you've attached from other places on FamilySearch, as well as sources you've manually uploaded. To add a source (such as a tombstone or cemetery document), click Add Source and enter the required information. Be as specific as possible.

STEP 5 Set up edit notifications. Because FamilySearch uses the "one tree" model for its family tree, anyone can edit any profile that has been made public. To receive a notification whenever someone edits this person's profile, click Watch underneath the ancestor's name at the top of the page.

KEYS from the CRYPT

• Upload your ancestor's tombstone information—plus any other burial information you have—to online databases such as Find A Grave, BillionGraves, and FamilySearch. This will help you pay tribute to your deceased relatives, and you never know who may be looking for the same ancestors!

• Volunteer to take and upload photos of local graves to online databases, and enroll in online transcription projects. Pitching in with these massive projects helps out other researchers and makes the whole effort more complete and accurate.

More Sites

- The Association for Gravestone Studies (AGS) <**www.gravestonestudies. org**>: This organization promotes the conservation, preservation, and education of gravestone studies in the United States.
- DeathIndexes.com <**www.deathindexes.com**>: This site provides searchable death records and indexes listed by state and county.
- Interment.net <**www.interment.net**>: This site lists million of records from thousands of cemeteries throughout the United States, Canada, the United Kingdom, and more.
- A Grave Interest <**agraveinterest.blogspot.com**>: My blog tells of anything and everything fascinating about cemeteries, from art, sculpture, architecture, bios of famous and not-so-famous people, and graveyard culture.
- Grave Hunter <**gravehunter.net**>: This has become what Find A Grave started as: a site for those seeking the famously departed.

8

Tombstone Transcription Form

Once you return from the cemetery, it's important to record everything you see on a tombstone. Use this form to transcribe all the information on your ancestor's grave marker.

Name	
Birth date	
Death date	
Marriage date	
Spouse name	
Relatives named	
Epitaph	
Location	
Notes about military service: rank, conflict(s) served, regiment, etc.	
Notes about symbols, tombstone shape and condition, etc.	

PART FOUR

DIGGING DEEPER

Other Records

B y now, you've done quite a bit of research online and in cemeteries for records of your ancestor's death. But dusty cemetery tombstones, weathered grave markers, and databases such as Find A Grave <**www.findagrave.com**> and BillionGraves <**www. billiongraves.com**> are just the first of several places to discover information about your ancestor's life. Genealogists make use of many kinds of death records that were created for a wide variety of reasons.

In this chapter, we'll discuss the records that you can't typically find on cemetery grounds, plus what each kind of record can provide for your research.

DEATH RECORDS

Death records are an abundant and important source for genealogists. Created at the time of death with information provided by a family member or someone who (hopefully) knew the deceased well, death records are part of a trio of vital records that document the most important (hence, "vital") events in a person's life: birth, marriage, and death.

In the United States, most death records are kept at the local, county, or state level, meaning you should look to these repositories to find copies of them. While death records are great sources of information, most states didn't require them to be kept until the late nineteenth and early twentieth centuries, and you'll find that different parts of the country have different levels of coverage. New England states, for example, have much better death records because their churches have been registering this information for over three hundred years, but researchers with ancestors in other parts of the country may have more difficulty.

Death records can lead you to investigate other files such as church documents, probate and court records, civil records, and Social Security forms. These documents provide valuable detail, including medical information that can help you identify diseases and disorders that are common in your lineage.

Death Certificates

Death certificates are the legal proof of an individual's death, kept by the government and filled out by a medical professional or coroner. These death records typically contain the most detail, mentioning the time, date, place, and cause of a person's death.

Throughout the past several decades, death certificates have become more common (and more detailed). Local counties may have kept records of who had died within their jurisdictions from early in their histories, but it wasn't until 1900 that widespread vital record-keeping became common in many states. Early death records contained little more than the deceased's name and date and place of death. Around 1910, death records began to contain facts about an individual's

GRAVE TIP

9

State Your Business: Usually, local or county offices can accommodate an inquiry faster than the state, so (if given the choice between the two) you should contact local offices first. And when requesting a death certificate, be sure to specify that you would like a *full* death certificate, as this can include much more detailed information than the shorter version. Also be prepared to show ID and verify your relationship to the deceased.

life and circumstances of his death, and by the mid-1930s, all states were collecting information about an individual's death. In later years, certificates began noting race, education, occupation, marital status, spouse's name, maiden name, birthplace, Social Security number, military service, and (if female) whether the deceased was pregnant at the time of death. You can also find place of last residence, occupation, parents' names, marital status, and the name of the informant and her relationship to the deceased.

Be on the lookout for erroneous information, especially in older records. While informants were usually in a good position to know details about the deceased, they may have been neighbors, friends, or in-laws with limited or imperfect knowledge. Even close relatives still could have been mistaken regarding specific facts. For example, my grandfather, Robert Dellinger, is listed as a truck driver on his death certificate, even though he and my grandma ran a poultry-processing business on their farm—the only truck Grandpa ever drove was a Ford pickup of various models. Why Grandpa's daughter (the informant) listed his occupation as truck driver, I don't know.

Transcription errors (for digitized records) and typos (for more recent records) also occur, and these can significantly throw off your

Leap of Faith: Religious Vital Records

Each religion has its own types of papers and records deemed important to that faith. The most prominent church records include baptism, christening, confirmation, and marriage (both certificates and banns), along with funeral and burial. Most of these records are kept in bound church books, but be sure to check for religious records in other places as well: membership lists, meeting minutes, lists of communicant/parish registers, church bulletins, church photos, newsletters, newspapers, or missals. Also search for tombstone inscriptions, pew rentals, bar/bat mitzvah records, published congregational histories, biographies of clergy or prominent church members, or church correspondence and other clergy papers. Churches also kept files on families that transferred their membership records when they moved away.

research. For example, my grandfather's death certificate lists him as dying on December 20, 1000. Always be prepared to back up these records with other documents, and be skeptical of other information until you can verify it for yourself.

Not everyone has a legal right to obtain a copy of a death certificate. Many records repositories impose a fifty-year stay on death certificates to protect the privacy of the deceased and their families. Those eligible usually include the spouse, children, siblings, or other direct-line descendants or relatives of the deceased with a documented medical need for the certificate.

Probate Records

Probate records, which include wills and estate records, are created as a person's estate is settled after death, including distributing the deceased's assets to heirs or creditors. If the deceased had a will (i.e., if he was testate), the court is to document the will's validity and oversee its implementation—and field concerns from people who wish to contest the will. If the deceased left no will (i.e., if she was intestate), the probate court appoints an administrator to decide the distribution of the deceased's assets according to the appropriate laws.

Probate records can list the names of the deceased's spouse, children, married daughters' spouses, and grandchildren, as well as:

- An inventory of the estate's assets
- A list of heirs, creditors, and debts (if any)

9

- The names of the executors (i.e., the people designated to put the will into action)
- Documentation of how assets (money, valuable possessions, real estate, etc.) should be distributed
- Petitions for guardianship of underage children
- The signatures and names of witnesses, possibly family members

Probate records can tell you a lot about your ancestors and their lifestyle. Did your great-great-great-great-grandfather leave his estate to his wife, or did he put a son in charge? Were provisions made to care for an ancestor's widow and underage children? Did all children inherit equally, or did the deceased favor one child over others? Did his daughters' inheritance pass into the care of their husbands? The answer to these questions gives you an intimate look into the family's structure and social and economic status.

Probate records will also show if the family was charitable in the community and to what organizations (churches, hospitals, political parties) contributions and assets were gifted. This can help you determine what religion and/or political party your ancestors supported, which can lead to more records.

Obituaries

Obituaries and death notices are favorite death records for genealogists because they're loaded with information and increasingly easy to locate. Thanks to the Internet, newspapers across the world are now placing their obituaries online for easy access, and recent advancements in optimized character recognition (OCR) technology are making them keyword-searchable. Older obituaries that aren't yet online may be accessed through a newspaper's archives or on microfilm at local libraries and universities.

Some obituaries contain only basic information about the deceased, while others may be lengthy biographical sketches detailing the decedent's life. An obituary usually lists:

- Full name of the deceased (often including a maiden name)
- Date, time, location, and cause of death

- Date and place of birth
- Name of spouse
- Names of children and their spouses, with places of residence
- Names of grandchildren, nieces, nephews, siblings, and (sometimes) former spouses
- Previous addresses
- Occupations
- Employers
- Military service
- Fraternal and club memberships
- Religious affiliation
- Funeral home in charge of arrangements
- Date and time of burial
- Cemetery of interment

At one time, a newspaper editor or reporter wrote the obituary, pulling information from previous publications and/or details provided by the family. In small communities, the publisher or editor might know the deceased firsthand, so could therefore write a detailed obituary. The undertaker could also be called upon to write the obituary from information provided by the family.

An obituary gives more personal information about the deceased than other kinds of records, such as death notices. Death notices are simple, straightforward announcements of a person's demise that give just the basic facts (no biographical information), including death date

9

GRAVE TIP

Learn the Lingo: Keep in mind that the medical terms we use today are not necessarily what our ancestors used. See our list of archaic disease names <www.familytreemagazine.com/article/name-that-ailment> and other online guides to learn more.

and time along with funeral location, date, and time. Depending on the relationship and financial situation, a family may decide to initially publish only a death notice.

Once you've found your ancestor's obituary, make a list of all the names and relationships mentioned (see chapter 8 for an example of a transcribed obituary), then figure out how these people are related to other members on your family tree. Keep in mind that spelling has changed in the past three hundred years, so deciphering an older obituary may be difficult.

Newspapers may have archived older obituaries. If not, check with the local library, historical organization, or genealogical society, as these groups could have records on microfilm. Contact state historical societies to see if the obituary has been published in a state genealogy periodical or abstract. Also look for newspapers published where the deceased was born or resided during an important part of his life. These papers may have been notified and crafted their own obituary based on what was known about the deceased when she resided there.

Obituaries, along with the publications they appeared in, are being digitized and indexed with increasing speed. For-pay databases such as Genealogy Bank <www.genealogybank.com> and Ancestry.com's Newspapers.com <www.newspapers.com> have made thousands of publications available to subscribers, and more titles are becoming searchable as OCR technology improves. Other free sites, such as FamilySearch.org <www.familysearch.org>, RootsWeb <www.rootsweb.org>, and USGenWeb <www.usgenweb.org>, also contain collections of obituaries.

Funeral Home Records

Funeral home records, also known as mortuary records, are yet another overlooked resource for the genealogy researcher. These documents contain the same basic information about the deceased as the death certificate, but offer more detailed family information including addresses, a copy of the obituary, possible insurance data, and financial records related to the cost of the funeral and burial. Mortuary records can also assist you in locating the cemetery and the burial records held there.

Funeral homes began keeping files in the late nineteenth and early twentieth centuries. Before that, the church held death records, and funerals, wakes, or remembrance events would have taken place in the parlor of the deceased's home. As the undertaker had a more active role in the embalming and burial process, memorial services and burial rites shifted to his establishment (known as the "funeral parlor"), and the name morphed into "funeral home" as fewer and fewer people had parlors in their homes. Besides keeping records and hosting services, the funeral director also became responsible for completing and filing the death certificate, working with an informant to gather the required data. The funeral director also writes and sends obituaries to media outlets.

Funeral home documents include the deceased's name, age, date and location of death, burial date, cemetery, officiating clergy, family informants, family members, and last address, plus a copy of an obituary and clippings from newspapers. Other records may include memorial cards and flower lists, along with a detailed list of funeral expenses or simply a sum total bill. If the invoice is detailed, you can also learn about the family's financial status.

To begin a search for records created by a funeral home that's in business, contact the establishment to make sure it still has the records. Schedule an appointment with a funeral director and let him know whose records you would like to review, including the date of death and any other information he may need to locate the files.

If a funeral home is no longer in business, check with other mortuaries in the area to see if the records were transferred or if another undertaker purchased the business. If not, visit the local or county genealogical or historical library and society to see if the records have been moved there or if someone knows what became of them. Many times, the director took the records with him for safekeeping when a funeral home closed.

Autopsies, Coroner's Reports, and Inquests

When our ancestors died, authorities may have created documents about the circumstances of their death, and these can be valuable resources for genealogists.

Specifically, a coroner (a medical professional trained in forensics and either elected or appointed by the government to the position) may perform an autopsy to determine a cause of death. An autopsy consists of an external exam of the body, both with and without clothing. The coroner looks for traumatic injuries and signs of disease. Physical evidence collected includes hair and nail clippings along with organs, tissues, and bodily fluids. The full autopsy is restricted to certain people: immediate family members and (if applicable) an insurance company.

Still, autopsies—if you can find them among family records—are of interest to genealogists because they can reveal heredity illness and if the death was caused by a work-related injury or by a disease not previously diagnosed.

Coroners reports, which summarize details from the autopsy and couple it with other documents related to the deceased's death, are more accessible, as they're available to the public. A coroner's report may be one page or several, depending on what the coroner was searching for, the reason for the investigation, and the actual findings. The report is made up of several records, including necrology reports (similar to obituaries), pathology reports, toxicology reports, police reports, testimony, and jury reports.

Coroners reports contain:
- Name, age, race, gender, and address of the deceased
- Location where the body was found
- Location where the death occurred (if different)
- Name of the person reporting the death
- Name of the person certifying the death
- Date and location of the autopsy
- Name of the coroner/medical examiner who performed the autopsy
- Probable cause of death
- Probable manner of death (natural, accident, suicide, homicide, undetermined)
- Probable mechanism of death (process by which vital organs failed)

These details can guide you to do more research in newspapers, court reports, hospital records, and police reports.

While autopsies and coroner's reports are produced if the cause of death is suspected to be unnatural, coroner's inquests are created when a death was not due to natural causes. This is a probing interrogation into how, what, when, where, and why the death occurred. Inquest records include the deceased's name, address, occupation, description, where and when the inquest was held, witnesses' names, jurors' names, and the verdict. Testimony at the inquest may include police statements and testimonies, along with photographs, suicide notes, and other items relevant to the case.

Don't forget to check local and regional newspapers to see if the inquest was mentioned. Most are public, so the newspapers can carry the basics unless the inquest is part of an ongoing murder trial. Early records may be found at the county courthouse in the county clerk's office. Also, check with the current coroner/medical examiner's office for suggestions on where old files are stored. And be sure to search the state archives.

OTHER GENEALOGY RECORDS

Records created to document a person's death will obviously contain information relevant to that event, but other kinds of genealogy records can still be crucial to researching your deceased ancestors. This section will provide a crash-course on other kinds of genealogy records that you should consult when researching your deceased ancestors.

9

City Directories

City directories are great for research because they link people to specific regions at certain periods of time. City directories were first developed for merchants, salesmen, and other professionals/companies who wanted to contact residents in certain towns. The first known directory, which would become the template for early city directories, was *A Directory for the City of New York in 1665*, which covered the newly colonized city of New York.

City directories were published annually and mainly included information on the male head-of-household: his name, address, spouse's name, and occupation. But they can tell us a lot about our ancestors and give us an historical perspective concerning our ancestors' lives, where they resided, and when. Since the directories were published once a year, these annual accounts of life can help fill in the gaps between the decennial census years. By utilizing city directories for each year our ancestor resided in this location, we get a more adequate picture of who he was, what he did for a living, where he worked, and the neighborhood he lived in.

And even though they generally only featured information about men, city directories can still tell you about the whole family's life. Other family members may be hiding in records of marriages, births, and deaths that occurred each year, and we can also follow a family as it left one town and moved to a new home elsewhere (or at least become aware that a family left the town, even if we don't know its destination). These directories are very useful when searching for someone new to the area, a family that was renting living space, or ancestors residing in the city temporarily. This may be the only place to locate those who didn't own land and were not registered to vote.

One of the most productive city directory publishing companies was R.L. Polk and Company, which published its first directory in 1872 for the city of Evansville, Indiana. By 1907, R.L. Polk and Company had expanded into producing gazetteer business directories, along with regional directories of post offices and banks. Other published directories included elite and social registers known as Blue Books.

A city directory typically has the following features:

- Alphabetical listing of residents
- Business index
- Crisscross section, allowing readers to look up information under more than one heading (the *Cole's Directory* in 1947 had the first)
- Ethnic listings (in directories that had separate sections for African-Americans, Jews, Asian-Americans, and other minority groups)

- Maps indicating the locations of churches, cemeteries, fraternal organizations, funeral homes, hospitals, post offices, and schools
- Social registers
- Street names
- Street locator maps

Originally, city directories only included the movers and shakers of the community. Later, the majority of the town was included. Unfortunately, certain parts of town were ignored due to racial or economic status.

As city directories became more popular (more than twelve thousand were published in total), they began to include more diverse information. City directories indicated who the head of the household was and (in many cases, in parentheses) his wife's name. If children worked outside the home, their names and occupations could be listed as well.

Besides recording names and addresses, a directory might also have the occupations of the head-of-household (later to include all residents), a reverse street directory, and a listing of local businesses and government institutions. Later directories also provided not only a person's occupation, but also his employer and what neighborhood he lived in.

Sometimes illustrations of businesses shops and factories were included, helpful when searching for local stores, churches, and schools the family may have patronized. Some directories were so complete that they even included the sunrise and sunset times for each day, along with stagecoach and steamboat arrival and departure times.

Directories, which were published annually, also began to include a section that noted additions, changes, and deletions from year to year. Pay special attention to these sections—the changes and deletions may be due to a death, which can help you narrow the date of death (i.e., when your ancestor disappeared from the directory). In a similar way, if your male ancestor's wife is suddenly listed as a widow in one year's directory, you have a good idea when her husband died.

9

Many directories also have an addendum that includes information received too late to put in its proper place. This could be due to people just moving to the city, or who were not home when the canvasser visited. By checking the appendix in the annual directory, you can learn the year your ancestors relocated to an area and even their date of immigration into the country.

You can also often use directories as gazetteers, since many include maps that show the location of schools, hospitals, fraternal organizations, clubs, associations, cemeteries, and churches. Reverse street listings listed street names alphabetically, making it easier to discover the names of the people living at each address. By using the address listed on death documents, you can locate where the deceased was living when she died. You can also use the address to locate tax records and property information.

If you've searched the city directory and can't locate your family, be sure to check the spelling and try different variations. Just as with census records, the names in city directories could be spelled incorrectly because the enumerator didn't ask for the spelling and simply wrote it down phonetically. Other directories allowed people to opt out of being included.

Maybe your ancestor settled in a nearby town, or possibly there is another location within the state with a similar-sounding name. For example, Illinois has both a *Palatine* and a *Palestine*. The names are often confused but the distance, between the two towns is 270 miles, which could help you decide which location was meant.

There's not central database for city directories, so you may have to search around. The Library of Congress is the single largest repository of city directories <**www.loc.gov**>. City directories are available at individual genealogical societies, historical societies, and local libraries. State libraries are great resources if you're checking several different cities at a time. Also look for directories at the local Family History Center, as the staff there can assist you in locating the directories you need and requesting the microfilm from the Family History Library in Utah.

Land records describe what property the deceased bought, owned, and sold, allowing genealogists to tie ancestors to certain locales at specific times. Other family members may be found living in the area or moving to the region.

Pay attention to whom the heirs sell parcels of property. Do they have the same surname, or the last name as wives or mothers in the extended family? Land records are made up of several documents. Let's take a closer look at deeds, homestead land grants, and military bounty land warrants.

DEEDS

Deeds, which make up the bulk of US land records, establish the ownership and legal transfer of property from one person to another. When land is sold, the seller signs a deed transferring ownership of the land to the buyer, indicating that the owner (such as your ancestor) owned property, and where that property was located. The deed will also list a purchase price and selling price; if not, the deed is known as a "deed of gift" and indicates that the land was gifted to the "buyer." Deeds are located at the courthouse in the county where the property is located.

One question to keep in mind when searching deeds: Were there several grantors (sellers) involved? These could be relatives who purchased land together, or heirs of an estate who wished to sell land they were not going to use. Both situations give you more relationships to explore.

HOMESTEAD LAND GRANTS

The federal Homestead Act was established in 1862 to encourage settlers to relocate to more than one billion acres of public-domain land in the western regions of the United States. Homestead grants usually allowed for any American (including freed slaves) to claim up to 160 acres of federal land for free, provided the settler live on the land and make improvements on it for five years.

While only 40 percent of settlers fulfilled the homestead requirements, the government archived most of the homestead requests that were filled out. These applications can contain the names of family members, neighbors, marriage and death certificates, citizenship applications, and affidavits, providing researchers with a wealth of family information. Begin your search with at the National Archives <**www. archives.gov**>.

MILITARY BOUNTY LAND WARRANTS

Bounty land warrants were originally offered as incentives for soldiers to serve in specific military conflicts: the Revolutionary War (1775–1783), the early Indian Wars (1775–1855), the War of 1812 (1812–1815), and the Mexican-American War (1846–1848). Military bounty lands were later given to soldiers as remuneration for serving their country in a broader "time of need." Bounty lands could be claimed by the soldier or by his heirs, but a warrant was not automatically issued; a soldier or his family had to file an application.

Soldiers were typically awarded a standard amount of public-domain land once they had met the eligibility requirements of their military service, but not all soldiers were awarded a land bounty. For example, Revolutionary soldiers and noncommissioned officers usually received one hundred acres while officers could receive up to five hundred acres, but not each of the two hundred thousand soldiers who fought in the Revolutionary War received a land bounty. If a warrant was granted, the veteran then applied for a land patent—the document that would grant him ownership of the land. Few veterans actually applied for a land warrant, and those who did usually sold or traded their warrants to others for the cash or for land in a more appealing location.

Bounty files contain all types information and records regarding your ancestor's military service, including pension documents and other correspondence. A land bounty warrant will include his name, age, and place of residence at the time of application, along with his rank, military unit, and period of service. If a widow applied for her husband's land warrant, the information gathered included her age, maiden name, and place of residence, plus the date and place of the couple's marriage. A file can contain up to two hundred pages of information, but a typical file has about thirty pages including the application, evidence of identity, service records, claims, and a decision on approval status.

More than eighty thousand of these forms have been placed on microfilm at the National Archives, and most of the records date from 1800 to 1900. (Files before 1800 were thought to have been destroyed in a fire in November 1800.) Most of these files involve the query of soldiers and families seeking to be granted a pension or land.

Locating land bounty warrants may take some time, but they can be extremely informative once you find them. Begin with the present day's state land office or historical society, then look in these large online databases:

- FamilySearch <www.familysearch.org> has a master listing of searchable records for the U.S. Revolutionary War Pension and Bounty Land Warrant Applications.
- RootsWeb <home.rootsweb.ancestry.com> is another free, reliable site.
- The National Archives offers a great pamphlet on Revolutionary War Pensions and Federal Land Bounty Warrants application files that give more history and details regarding what was involved <www.archives.gov/files/research/microfilm/m804.pdf>
- Several paid sites such as Ancestry.com, Heritage Quest <www.heritagequestonline.com> (which has free access at some libraries), and Fold3 <www.fold3.com> offer an actual look at warrant applications online.

When searching, remember that some modern state boundaries have changed since your ancestor applied for bounty. "Virginia" bounty land, for example, was located in today's states of Kentucky and Ohio, while records for Maine may be held in Massachusetts. Be sure you're searching in the correct state.

Court Records

Court records document legal proceedings that took place due to a violation or dispute of law. Ancestors may have been called into court as witnesses, plaintiffs, defendants, or jurors, and records can include names, genders, race, ages, martial statuses, occupations, and addresses.

While records can be difficult to locate due to changes in court names and jurisdictions, don't be dissuaded from trying.

When searching for court records, begin by researching these three types:

EQUITY CASES

Equity cases do not involve any violations of the law, but are based in disputes and arguments between individuals, such as property rights, estate probates, adoptions, or divorce proceedings. Equity cases are tried in county and local courts, and records can be found in the town's courthouse or at the local repository for legal historical archives. (Note: Modern equity cases are now tried in civil court, so more recent records will be found in civil court proceedings.)

CIVIL CASES

Civil cases involve the alleged wrongdoing by one individual (or party) against another. They include charges of libel, property damage, or domestic violence, and plaintiffs sue to protect an individual's private rights or to request retribution in the form of monetary compensation for a violation of rights. Civil cases are usually tried in state court systems according to state laws and statutes, and you can find records at county courthouses, state archives, or state genealogical societies.

CRIMINAL CASES

Criminal cases are brought forward when individuals break the law or society is otherwise harmed by an individual's actions. Criminal cases include sex crimes, involuntary manslaughter, and murder, and the state (which represents "the people") files a lawsuit against an individual. Crimes vary in severity, with distinctions between a felony (a serious charge carrying possible jail time) and a misdemeanor (a less serious crime with no jail time). Criminal court cases are usually tried in state courts according to the state constitution and laws, or (if the crime involved a violation of federal statutory laws or the US Constitution) in federal court.

Local and state criminal records can be found at the appropriate courthouses. The location of federal court records will depend on the time frame of the court case. Check Public Access to Court Electronic Records (PACER) to get started <**www.uscourts.gov/courtrecords/ find-case-pacer**>.

Institutional Records

It's always interesting to imagine our ancestors' lives. Were they business people in the community, or were they sage farmers, toiling from daylight to dusk? Were they rule-abiding citizens, or lawbreakers with a record? Only records can tell. Ah, there's the rub—those highly sought-after records are sometimes hard to find. Institutional records—documents from schools, hospitals, orphanages, almshouses, and prisons—can provide insight into some of these questions, simply because they gathered different information than other kinds of records.

Institutions are organizations that govern the behaviors of a specific group of people, all with something in common: prisoners, veterans, children, and the poor. These specific groups of records are intertwined and usually lead back to other records and reports.

Every level of government maintains institutions. The federal branch houses veterans homes and hospitals, along with federal penitentiaries, while states manage (state) prisons, hospitals, asylums, and institutions for the mentally disabled. Local governments oversee orphanages, almshouses, schools, and jails.

Institutions are wonderful at generating research leads. If you search for records at a veterans home, those files could lead you back to records about military service and fraternal organizations. By checking documents for hospitals, medical history becomes clearer and could aid you in understanding your family's health and genetic disposition. School documents may lead to orphanage records and church or charitable groups. Prison records indicate the types of crimes and age of offenders, and they can lead to court records and possibly newspaper accounts.

Government-directed institutions were historically better at recordkeeping than private companies. Luckily for us, document-purging schedules were not always closely followed, so you can still

9

find records, albeit not without some challenges. Privacy laws affect who is allowed to view records. Some government institutions have established time frames when information may be made available to the public—if ever. For example, the federal census records cannot be released to the public until seventy-two years after the census was taken in order to keep personally identifiable information about individuals private for most, if not all, their lives. The seventy-two-year rule restricts access to census records to all but the individuals named in the records and their legal heirs.

Private institutions have fewer regulations concerning paperwork, which means those records may have been destroyed or stored in a location that no one now remembers. Either situation is bad news for the genealogist. Private companies can also deny anyone the right to view the records, and there is no legal recourse to appeal the decision.

Trying to find these records can be difficult. Here are nine places to check for these elusive documents:

1. The institution in question and the organization that runs/ran it—if it still exists
2. Local and county historical societies
3. Local and regional libraries and universities
4. State historical groups
5. State libraries
6. State archives (for records from state institutions)
7. Headquarters of fraternal organizations
8. Headquarters of religious bodies
9. Online collections made in partnership with any of the above

SCHOOLS

Educational records tell us more about our ancestor than just her name, age, and grade. These are documents that can make an individual "come alive" in our minds. Just by looking at her report card, we know what subjects our ancestor excelled at, and what she didn't care for.

Educational records include:

- Administrative agendas
- Attendance log books

- Class photos
- Class yearbooks
- Indexes of teachers and principals
- Report cards
- School board meeting minutes
- Student lists
- School newspapers

When researching a student from the distant past, keep in mind that children raised on farms didn't attend school on the same schedule as city kids. Rural children also had to help with the planting in the spring and the harvest in the autumn, so they would only attend school during the winter months. Many children dropped out of school at a young age to help support the family by apprenticing or working in factories, and this could have been noted in the teacher's class journal.

Educational institutions can include elementary, middle, and high schools, along with trade schools, colleges, and professional schools. Other schools include preparatory, boarding, and military academies. There were also ethnic schools for Native American, African-American, Jewish, and Asian children.

As schools became integrated during the 1960s, race was still a factor that was listed in educational records, sometimes in covert ways, such as the color of paper used to document the child's records. Unfortunately, microfilmed documents in black and white do not share this bit of clandestine history with the researcher.

University documents can hold information about the student's family from admission records. Other information includes the main course of study, grades received, personal biographies printed in college newspapers and yearbooks, groups and associations the student belonged to, graduation dates, and alumni information.

When searching for educational records, contact the state archives or visit the National Archives for relevant school forms. Yearbooks may be found at local historical societies or libraries, plus at the school library (if the school still exists).

ORPHANAGES

Orphanages were set up in the United States during the eighteenth and nineteenth centuries to care for children who had been abandoned or whose parents had died. Orphanages were operated by religious organizations, charities, private contributors, and local and state governments. As states took over orphanages, provisions and policies began to differ widely.

Orphanages were particularly crowded from the end of the Civil War until the end of the Great Depression. In 1909, the White House Conference on the Care of Dependent Children suggested that children who could not be cared for in their homes should be placed in foster homes, but it was not until after World War II that traditional orphanages either converted into group homes or closed their doors.

Orphanages operated by local and state governments kept detailed records and had appointed overseers who investigated the homes for cleanliness, food, and education. Those run by religious organizations, private groups, and charities also kept good records, but those records became difficult to locate once the orphanages were closed.

Orphanage records include the child's name, age, birthplace, date of birth, name of parents, date of admission, and date of discharge, plus whether the child was orphaned or abandoned. Other information may be found in the "Matron's Report," which details a day-to-day existence at the orphanage—who was ill, who visited, who was admitted, and why. The "Manager's Book" is also worth a look for administrative figures, health reports, finances, and other business-related data. Records for government-run orphanages may be accessible through the state's archives. For records from orphanages operated by non-governmental entities, check with state and local historical societies. If a religious organization ran the home, request record books and information from the headquarters.

HOSPITALS

Early hospital and doctor records list everything from the patient's information (name, age, date of admission, disease, and date of death) to treatments used, with special notations if the disorder was hereditary in nature. Tuberculosis sanitariums, in particular, were usually run by the state in the late nineteenth and early twentieth centuries to combat "consumption," which was taking a heavy toll across the country.

When starting a search for hospital records, find out how long medical records must be kept by the state where the facility is/was located. The number of years can vary.

Unfortunately, finding the hospital where your ancestor sought treatment may prove a challenge, since early medial facilities changed names, closed down, and moved. If the hospital is gone, search for public hospital records through the state's medical board, or visit the National Archives and search for medical treatment records. Documents kept by hospitals that are still in operation may be considered confidential records, so gaining access to them could be difficult unless the specified time frame has elapsed.

POORHOUSES/POOR FARMS

In the nineteenth century, the indigent were sent to live in poorhouses, institutions on "poor farms" that provided housing and employment for the destitute, those without work or who could not work, and those who had no where else to turn. A poorhouse was run by the country government and supported with public tax money. Food and housing were provided in exchange for residents working on the farm—cleaning house, doing laundry, and raising vegetables, grain, and livestock to be consumed by those who lived there. Strict rules governed the establishment.

Poorhouse records provide a stark look at what life was like in these institutions. Documents include the name of each resident, along with each person's age, race, township, date admitted, cause for admitting and by whose order, and date discharged. If the person died while in a poorhouse, the documents also note his date of death, cause of death, and location of burial, plus any other remarks.

Poorhouse records may be found at state archives, or by contacting the county courthouse to locate annual town or county reports for the specified time period. During the 1930s and 1940s, the Works Progress Administration (WPA) inventoried numerous county archives. Check with the county where the poor farm was located to see if the WPA kept local poorhouse records.

FRATERNAL ORGANIZATIONS

Hundreds of fraternal groups and organizations in the United States at the turn of the twentieth century brought people together through service, religion, military experience, or business interests in what was called "the Golden Age of Fraternalism." And these groups took their membership seriously and kept exceptional records.

Organization and lodge records contain members' names, dates of acceptance, levels of rank attained, and offices held. These groups include the Freemasons, the Independent Order of Odd Fellows, the Knights of Pythias, the Benevolent and Protective Order of Elks, the Improved Order of Red Men, and the Ancient Order of United Workmen, to name just a few. These groups may also have built and run homes for the widowed and elderly, orphanages, and hospitals. Many had their own cemeteries in which members were buried, and (as we discussed in chapter 6) gravestones may bear the fraternal organization's logo or mark as a way of identifying the deceased as a member of this elite group. Try contacting the organization's headquarters with the member's name and other identifying information to request records.

Your ancestors may have also joined a fraternal benefit society, a voluntary association formed to provide a mutual benefit—usually insurance—to its members. For example, the Modern Woodmen of America and the Woodmen of the World were both founded by Joseph Cullen Root in the late 1800s to make life insurance available to working men and their families.

Details pertaining to the family, their policy, and any benefits paid would contain a wealth of information for the genealogist: names of the members and their families, dates (and causes) of death, and information about the value of the family's property.

PRISONS

Prison records are a gold mine of information. Although the initial discovery of having a jailbird in the family might be scandalous, this is one of the best-kept and most detailed record systems in the country.

The first prison in the United States was established in 1773 in Philadelphia. The federal prison system was established in the 1890s, and early offenders were convicted of "crimes" that today our society would consider to be minor violations.

The information that prison records include will differ according to the penitentiary and what entity had authority over it, but here are several to search for:

- Admission records: Documents created when an inmate was committed to a prison, often including the inmate's name, date of admission, race, gender, health, family diseases, number of convictions, length of sentence, etc.
- Applications for clemency: An appeal for mercy granted by state governor or president
- Biographical registers: Information on inmates and their families
- Convict docket sheets: Inmate's name, crime, sentence, date sentenced, when discharged
- Death warrants: Official authorization to carry out an execution
- Discharge books: Inmate's name, date of discharge, age, race, gender, time in prison, physical and mental health status at time of release, and pardon information
- Execution lists: Inmate's name, age, race, birthdate, method, drug protocol, and years from sentence to execution
- Hospital records: Information about the inmate's medical treatment
- Pardon book: List of inmates forgiven of their crimes by the government
- Petition for commutation: Request to reduce sentence
- Prison registers: Inmate's name, age, gender, weight, eye color, race, crime, physical description, education, marital status, personal habits, etc.

There are four jurisdictions that control prisons: federal, state, local, and military. You can locate a currently operating prison by searching the Federal Bureau of Prisons website **<www.bop.gov>**. When searching for records from a prison that is no longer in operation, contact the state's department of corrections, the state's archives, or the National Archives for assistance in tracking down the required documents.

WORKS PROGRESS ADMINISTRATION (WPA)

In May 1933, with the country in the throes of the Great Depression, President Franklin D. Roosevelt signed an executive order creating the WPA. From this agency stemmed the Historical Records Survey (HRS), which provided needed employment to historians, librarians, researchers, and clerical workers. Placed in regional, state, and district divisions, these workers were to collect, identify, survey, index, and conserve any historical records found in state, county, and local archives throughout the United States. Some of the information gathered was compiled into books of historical information.

Thanks to the HRS, the archives of courthouses, town halls, and vital statistic offices were recorded and inventoried from all (then) forty-eight states. Of the information collected, here are just a few highlights for the genealogist:

- Indexes to newspapers
- Vital statistics (county birth, marriage, and death records)
- Inventories of church records
- Cemetery lists
- Manuscripts found in private collections and libraries
- Historical indexes of slaves, Native Americans, and immigrants
- County courthouse records
- Naturalization catalogues
- Maritime records
- Portraits of public building files
- Federal and state census indexes
- Soundex for US census forms for several states from the late nineteenth century

Most of the work done by the HRS was either bound in book form or copied onto microfilm and placed in local libraries and archives, along with college libraries and other designated federal depositories. Unfortunately, some of the gathered work was never organized, thanks to a shutdown by Congress in February 1939. Congressmen feared Communists were being employed by "such artistic groups," including the HRS.

Because of the WPA and its HRS branch, an untold number of records were saved, indexed, archived, and kept for future generations, and today that information—if you can find it—is a boon to genealogists and historians. The government didn't set up a process when the HRS was terminated, so the records were not sent to one major location. Instead, the records were scattered around communities and states and today can be found in a variety of places. State archives and the National Archives house a majority of the information gleaned by the Historical Records Survey.

Begin your research for HRS records locally. Since the records were never well organized, they were placed in boxes and file cabinets and stored out of the way for future generations—tucked away in basements and attics across the United States. Many local libraries, historical societies, and universities became the custodians of theses files, so be sure to ask around.

If local groups did not have room, the records were usually boxed up and sent to the state's historical society or state library. Most state historians realized this information could be useful some day, and thankfully (since it seems to go against an historian's nature to toss things away) many were preserved. As a result, you may need only a few calls to discover where the records were sent, either regionally or to the state capitol.

On a national level, the National Archives has a large collection of WPA and HRS records, with over 1,400 pages on file. You may also request information on the WPA researcher who worked on gathering the information in your area, then request his or her personnel files. And because the National Archives have branch offices across the country, you don't necessarily have to go to Washington, D.C. to view records; simply request they be sent to the district office in your region. Learn more about these records on the National Archives site. Likewise, the Library of Congress has its own collection of HRS and WPA records <www.loc.gov/manuscripts/?q=wpa>.

 ## KEYS from the CRYPT

• Continue your research beyond the cemetery for other kinds of death and burial records, such as civil death certificates, religious death records, obituaries, funeral home records, and more.

• Branch out to investigate other kinds of resources (such as city directories, court cases, school class photos, probate records, and fraternal organizations) to discover more about your deceased ancestors.

Records Checklist

You can find information about your ancestors in a wide variety of genealogical records. Use the checklist on the next two pages to keep track of which resources you've consulted.

Federal census

Search each US census taken during your ancestor's lifetime. Due to the different information collected from census to census, search each census collection individually to utilize search parameters available only for that census. Federal censuses were taken every ten years. Currently available collections include censuses from 1790 to 1940. (Note: The 1890 census contains only a fragment of the records due to water damage following a fire.)

☐ 1940	☐ 1900	☐ 1860	☐ 1820
☐ 1930	☐ 1890	☐ 1850	☐ 1810
☐ 1920	☐ 1880	☐ 1840	☐ 1800
☐ 1910	☐ 1870	☐ 1830	☐ 1790

Vital records

Drill down to the records relating specifically to your ancestor's place of birth, marriage, and death. Use search filters to narrow by collection and find individual collections to search. Start with death records and work your way backwards. Death records often contain more information that will help you than other vital records.

BIRTH AND DEATH RECORDS

☐ birth certificates
☐ death certificates
☐ Social Security Death Index
☐ obituaries and death announcements in newspapers
☐ burial and grave records
☐ wills
☐ probate court records

9

MARRIAGE AND DIVORCE RECORDS

- ☐ marriage bonds, licenses, and certificates
- ☐ engagement, wedding, or anniversary announcements in newspapers
- ☐ divorce records

CHURCH RECORDS

- ☐ baptism/christening record
- ☐ marriage banns/records
- ☐ burial records

Other records

Many other records collections may have information on your ancestors or the areas and time periods in which they lived.

MILITARY

- ☐ draft, enlistment, and service records
- ☐ soldier, veteran, and prisoner rolls and lists
- ☐ pension records
- ☐ regimental histories

IMMIGRATION AND TRAVEL

- ☐ passenger and ship crew lists
- ☐ border crossing records and passports
- ☐ naturalization records
- ☐ federal census records

PUBLICATIONS

- ☐ newspapers
- ☐ genealogical periodicals
- ☐ compiled genealogies (family histories, biographies)
- ☐ American Genealogical-Biographical Index
- ☐ oral histories and interviews
- ☐ local and county histories
- ☐ church histories
- ☐ school lists and yearbooks
- ☐ city and area directories
- ☐ telephone directories
- ☐ professional and organizational directories
- ☐ maps, atlases, and gazetteers

LAND RECORDS

- ☐ deeds
- ☐ bounty land warrants
- ☐ homestead records
- ☐ land grants and patents

LEGAL RECORDS

- ☐ tax lists
- ☐ criminal lists/criminal case files
- ☐ convict/prisoner records
- ☐ court records
- ☐ guardianship papers

NON-FEDERAL CENSUS RECORDS

- ☐ state and local censuses
- ☐ voter registration lists

9

Preserving Cemeteries

We often refer to things that have been finalized as being "set in stone," as if stone was somehow a permanent fixture for ideas or text. Unfortunately, that's not the case—wind, rain, and time erode away at even the most resilient stones, and these natural processes can spell disaster for tombstone tourists hoping to always have these beautiful headstones in their communities.

In this chapter, we'll discuss why we need to preserve our cemeteries, as well as examine the different types of tombstones and how to care for them. I'll also share some preservation societies and organizations that you can get involved with should you want to take cemetery preservation to the next level.

WHY SAVE GRAVESTONES?

There are many cemeteries across this country—in fact, throughout the world—that are in desperate need of preservation. Cemeteries hold our ancestors' histories and give us the opportunity to come as close as we can to our past. If you've ever stood at the grave of an ancestor, you know what I mean. There is a pull, a feeling that these are *my people* that cannot be duplicated by any genealogical form or record. And it only occurs in a graveyard.

Cemeteries are more than just the places where we bury our dead. A cemetery is also a repository of life—our history, culture, and social norms—and intriguing archives of religious and genealogical information. Cemeteries are also cultural archives where our family's history, and that of the region, state, and country, survives uninterrupted (we hope) for the telling of our stories. As a tombstone tourist, I think graveyards are like museums with rarely seen sculpture, intricate carvings, and amazing architecture in a tranquil outdoor setting. What a perfect reason to explore our historic cemeteries and discover ways to preserve those that have been abandoned, forgotten, or damaged.

Even setting aside the personal and cultural significance of tombstones, a burial ground is also a green space filled with wildlife and birds, plus an arboretum that includes rare and unique plants and trees. In some places, such as big cities, cemeteries are the last pieces of (relatively) undeveloped land in an urban jungle, making them places for quiet reflection and oneness with nature. In short: A cemetery is an exquisite place of quiet reprieve where history whispers all around us.

Common Threats to Cemeteries

Unfortunately, many things threaten cemeteries and burial grounds: neglect, abandonment, vandalism, difficult access, insufficient funds, improper development, and even the well-intentioned attempts to repair historical stones without the necessary equipment and know-how. If our society does not step up and demand tougher laws concerning inappropriate real estate development along with regulations to protect abandoned, neglected, or mismanaged cemeteries, we will continue to lose some of the most beautiful and poignant examples of our history and culture.

Grave markers can be damaged in numerous ways. If a cemetery has been neglected or abandoned, vines and plants will grow unrestricted and eventually overwhelm the gravestones (images **A** and **B**).

Weather and the elements can do remarkable damage to cemetery stones, too, especially those made from sandstone, slate, limestone, and marble. See chapter 5 and the headstones section later in this chapter for more on how the weather can affect tombstones.

Image A: Weeds and tall grass can quickly overtake an abandoned cemetery.

Image B: Plants, trees, and other foliage can even take over massive monuments, like this mausoleum that's barely visible.

Image C: Some gravestone damage is man-made. Here, vandals have knocked over headstones.

Image D: Thieves pried the panel from this white bronze monument looking for hidden riches inside.

10

Another major threat to cemeteries, both in rural and city locations, is vandals. These hoodlums damage stones by toppling over markers (image **C**) or prying emblems off white bronze monuments searching for money or other "hidden treasures" stashed inside (image **D**). (People were almost never buried with treasures. The old adage "You can't take it with you" is accurate for the vast majority of people.)

Cemetery Responsibilities

Cemeteries are abandoned or "die" because there is no one left to care for them. This is usually the case in small family cemeteries or private, church, or organizational cemeteries. A cemetery may also be abandoned because of lack of money. If an older cemetery has reached capacity and has no perpetual care funds to assist with the maintenance of the grounds or stones, an owner may simply walk away and leave the site unattended.

Given that, who's responsible for the upkeep, maintenance, and preservation of a cemetery? It's an issue that can be concerning and confusing. Traditionally, a cemetery's responsibilities include the allotment and maintenance of the ground used for burials and for grave preparation. In reality, whoever is paying property taxes on the cemetery ground is the individual, corporation, or entity that is responsible for maintaining it. Groups that can own a cemetery include corporations, churches, towns, cities, townships, counties, and states. Laws differ depending on the group or government agency that controls the burial ground.

Regulations governing cemetery maintenance vary from state to state. In Indiana, for example, a township owning a cemetery must keep the ground level and fenced. Weeds must be pulled, debris picked up, and leaning tombstones straightened. But if a town, city, or county owns the cemetery, Indiana has no laws that describe how that cemetery should be maintained or preserved.

Owners of an active cemetery (one that is still being used for burials) are generally in charge of its maintenance. If the cemetery is privately owned, the church, organization, or family that controls it should perform maintenance. But many times these cemeteries have been forgotten and abandoned. In these cases, to whom does the responsibility of

10

upkeep fall? In the state of South Carolina, the family and descendants are expected to care for the individual graves of their ancestors. The state of Michigan designates the ownership of its cemeteries, with signs naming the entity in charge of the property. If a small cemetery has been abandoned in Michigan, it becomes the property of the current landowner. The Illinois Cemetery Care Act distinguishes between two types of cemeteries in the state: licensed (i.e., under state jurisdiction and so required to be maintained) and exempt (i.e., sites owned by non-profit groups that the state cannot control).

How can you locate the owner of a cemetery? Many times an inquiry at the local town, village, city or township hall, or county clerk's office will produce the owner's name. The county recorder of deeds or the county assessor's office can provide a legal description of the property.

HOW TO HELP

Many cemeteries don't have the resources to maintain their grounds adequately, and most of the cemeteries in need of some type of preservation are small. These sites are usually privately owned, or owned by a small village or town that can no longer afford their upkeep or repairs. Because of this, volunteers are the lifeblood of preservation. However, volunteers must do so in the least-damaging manner possible.

Cemetery preservation can include anything from documenting a graveyard for posterity to seeking historical and national designations as landmarks or registered historical sites to repairing and restoring historic markers. Cemetery upkeep is also necessary to maintain an appealing site; mending fences, cutting grass, and picking up debris are all vital elements in caring for the property.

Preserving a cemetery takes money, man-hours, and the skills necessary to accomplish these goals. Most states offer free preservation workshops, and a cemetery preservation guide may be available from the state's historical preservation agency. But remember, there are varying levels of skills needed to perform cemetery stone preservation.

Repairing historic grave markers properly is very difficult. Most repairs are complicated and require a professional—and this is not

10

Images E and F: Good intentions have often done more harm than good when trying to repair damaged tombstones, such as applying metal brackets or concrete fillings.

a time to skimp on the help or correct supplies. Although the stones shown in images **E** and **F** have been "fixed," they were not repaired in the correct manner and have compromised the original headstones.

For the best results, contact a preservation or restoration group that is trained and approved in the restoration field for assistance and/or a consultation.

If you discover an abandoned or neglected cemetery, or one that is being misused or destroyed, notify city, state, and government officials about its location. By alerting leaders of its existence, the parties responsible for its upkeep can be contacted, or the authorities (if no entity exists) can find the funding necessary to protect it.

For those who want to "care for" an ancestor's grave, there are several things you can do. Start by grabbing that cemetery bag from chapter 4 so you'll have the necessary supplies with you. Start by removing any debris that has lodged around the stone. Clip any grass that is getting unruly, and pull any weeds that are infringing on the stone. (Make sure these are weeds and not flowers someone has placed on the grave next door.) Take that spray bottle of water and a soft cloth to clean the gravestone of any bird droppings, or just to give it an nice dusting off.

You can also use a soft paintbrush to "sweep" away any mowed grass or accumulated dust and dirt off the marker.

However, if you find small rocks on the gravestone, leave them there. This likely mean someone has been paying their respects, and this is an old custom still practiced by many: bestowing a token of affection upon the deceased, and letting those passing by know this person is still loved and cared for.

If you have family buried far from where you live, consider hiring a company that provides gravesite concierge services such as edging, cleaning, and laying flowers. This is another way to give peace of mind to family members that their loved ones graves are still being tended and treasured.

As Benjamin Franklin so poignantly said, "Show me your burial grounds and I'll show you a measure of the civility of a community." It is in society's best interest to keep our cemeteries well-maintained and cared for, for they are the archives of our past and the chronicles of today, which will communicate who we are to future generations.

PRESERVATION SOCIETIES AND ORGANIZATIONS

Cemeteries are national treasures and should be treated as such. Numerous preservation organizations understand this and are great repositories for why, how, and where to seek assistance in preserving and maintaining a cemetery.

Here's a list of groups and associations that can provide you with more information and ideas:

- American Institute for Conservation for Historic and Artistic Works (AIC) <www.conservation-us.org>: The AIC is the only organization of its kind committed to preserving cultural materials. Started in 1972, the AIC is now the largest institution to work with conservation scientists, educators, archivists, and art historians to save our cultural treasures. The organization offers workshops and educational courses along with publications and resources, including a current list of conservation professionals.

10

Several of the AIC's specialty subgroups pertain to cemetery and gravestone preservation.

- **Association for Gravestone Studies (AGS) <www. gravestonestudies.org>**: Founded in 1977, the AGS is an organization that champions public awareness and appreciation for gravestones and cemeteries. AGS encourages the public to study gravestones for their artistic and historical value. The association offers publications, conferences, exhibits, and workshops that deal with conservation and historical significance of grave markers of all periods and styles.
- National Center for Preservation Technology and Training (NCPTT) **<www.ncptt.nps.gov>**: The NCPTT is under the umbrella of the National Parks Service. It promotes scientific and technological solutions for preserving historic artifacts in the fields of archeology, architecture, and landscape architecture, along with materials conservation. The group offers various resources related to cemetery conservation, plus research, education, and partnership opportunities. For a list of state historic preservation officers that may be able to offer assistance or advice, visit **<www.nps.gov/ nr/shpolist.htm>**.
- National Preservation Institute (NPI) **<www.npi.org>**: Founded in 1980, the NPI offers educational seminars and professional training for those involved in the preservation, management, and stewardship of cultural heritage.
- National Trust for Historic Preservation (NTHP) **<savingplaces. org>**: The NTHP, a subsidiary of the National Park Service, fights to protect historic buildings, neighborhoods, and landscapes. The organization has several slide shows available for educational purposes, along with blog posts that go into more depth about cemetery preservation.
- Saving Graves **<www.savinggraves.org>**: Saving Graves strives to educate and network with people interested in restoring, protecting, and preserving historic cemeteries. The organization works to preserve and protect human burial sites from unauthorized and unwarranted disturbance.

10

Also check with your state government to find out what associations work for the protection of cemeteries in your area.

It is our responsibility as citizens, historians, and genealogists to assist in the preservation of cemeteries. These "gateways to the past" provide us with amazing cultural resources, a wealth of historical assets, and valued public landscapes. They are worth protecting and preserving for future generations!

 KEYS from the CRYPT

• Understand the threats facing cemeteries and what people/organizations are in charge of maintaining them.

• Follow the first rule of gravestone preservation: Do no harm. Take only pictures in a cemetery, and leave only footprints.

• Save tombstone repairs for the professionals. Instead, become active in cemetery preservation organizations.

10

Worksheets

Cemetery research is just the tip of the genealogy iceberg. As you dive deeper into your family's history, the amount of information you find can be overwhelming. Use the worksheets in this section to help you organize and share your information.

In this section, you'll find:

- **Family Group Sheet:** Save information about a single-family unit.
- **Ancestor Worksheet:** Record a host of information about one individual family member.
- **Five-Generation Ancestor Chart:** Document your family back to your great-great-grandparents.
- **Research Repository Worksheet:** Plan trips to archives, cemeteries, and other record-holding locations.
- **Source Citation Worksheet:** Track where you got your research with this template for recording information about your sources.

Family Group Sheet

of the _____Family

Husband

Source #

Full name _____   _____

Birth date _____Place _____   _____

Marriage date _____Place _____   _____

Death date_____Place _____   _____

    Burial_____   _____

His father _____   _____

His mother with maiden name _____   _____

Wife

Full name _____   _____

Birth date _____Place _____   _____

Death date_____Place _____   _____

    Burial_____   _____

Her father _____   _____

Her mother with maiden name _____   _____

Other Spouses

Full name _____   _____

    Marriage date and place _____   _____

Full name _____   _____

    Marriage date and place _____   _____

Children of this marriage	Birth date and place	Death and burial dates and places	Spouse and marriage date and place

Ancestor Worksheet

Full Name (maiden name for women): _____

Social Security Number: _____

Nicknames and Alternate Names: _____

Surname Spelling Variations: _____

Birth and Baptism

Birth Date: _____ Birth Place: _____

Baptism Date: _____ Baptism Place: _____

Marriage(s) and Divorce(s)

Name of Spouse(s)	Marriage Date(s)	Marriage Place(s)

Name of Spouse(s)	Divorce Date(s)	Divorce Place(s)

Death

Death Date: _____ Death Place: _____

Burial Date: _____ Burial Church/Place: _____

Obituary Date(s) and Newspaper(s): _____

Military Service

Conflict (if applicable)	Unit	Dates/Years

Migration

From	To	Departure/ Arrival Dates	Companion(s)	Ship (if applicable)

Personal Information

Schools Attended: _____

Religion Church(es) Attended: _____

Hobbies Club Memberships: _____

Children

Child's Name	Birth Date	Birthplace	Other Parent

Friends, Witnesses, and Neighbors to Research

Name	Relationship

Five-Generation Ancestor Chart

4

birth date and place

marriage date and place

death date and place

2

birth date and place

marriage date and place

death date and place

5

birth date and place

death date and place

1

birth date and place

marriage date and place

death date and place

spouse

6

birth date and place

marriage date and place

death date and place

3

birth date and place

death date and place

7

birth date and place

death date and place

Chart # ___
1 on this chart =___ on chart #___

see chart #

16

8 _____

17

birth date and place

marriage date and place

death date and place

18

9 _____

19

birth date and place

death date and place

20

10 _____

21

birth date and place

marriage date and place

death date and place

22

11 _____

23

birth date and place

death date and place

24

12 _____

25

birth date and place

marriage date and place

death date and place

26

13 _____

27

birth date and place

death date and place

28

14 _____

29

birth date and place

marriage date and place

death date and place

30

15 _____

31

birth date and place

death date and place

Research Repository Worksheet

Name of repository: _____

Address/Directions	
Hours (Closed for Lunch?)	
Holidays closed	
Name of contact person	
Cost of photocopies	
Restrictions on photocopying	
Change machine or cashier?	
Nearest places to park (with cost)	
Nearest places to eat	
Local lodging	
Handicap access?	
Research restrictions (Briefcases/laptops allowed? Lockers available?	
Any records stored off site? If so, how can they be accessed?	

Source Citation Worksheet

Source type (book, manuscript, type of record, etc.)	
Source format (microfilm, original, printed copy, etc.)	
Author or creator's name (agency, department, person)	
Title of work	
Date of work	
Publication place and publisher	
Collection or series name	
Box and folder	
Page number	
Repository	
Date viewed	
Notes on condition	

More Resources

Books

African American Historic Burial Grounds and Gravesites of New England, by Glenn A. Knoblock (McFarland, 2015)

A Graveyard Preservation Primer (American Association for State and Local History) 2nd Edition, by Lynette Strangstad (Rowman & Littlefield Publishers, 2013)

The American Resting Place: 400 Years of History Through Our Cemeteries and Burial Grounds, by Marilyn Yalom and Reid S. Yalom (Houghton Mifflin Harcourt, 2008)

The Archaeology of American Cemeteries and Gravemarkers (American Experience in Archaeological Perspective), by Sherene Baugher and Richard Veit (University Press of Florida, 2016)

Beautiful Death: The Art of the Cemetery, by Dean Koontz (Penguin Studio, 1996)

Beyond Grief: Sculpture and Wonder in the Gilded Age Cemetery, by Cynthia Mills (Smithsonian Institution Scholarly Press, 2015)

Beyond the Dark Veil: Post Mortem & Mourning Photography from The Thanatos Archive, by Jack Mord (Last Gasp, 2014)

Cemetery Art & Symbolism in North America, by D.A. Goodrich (CreateSpace Independent Publishing Platform, 2015)

Cemetery and Funeral Home Research Records: A Family Tree Research Workbook (Family Tree Workbook) (Volume 4), by Catherine Coulter (CreateSpace Independent Publishing Platform, 2013)

Cemeteries and Gravemarkers: Voices of American Culture, edited by Richard E. Meyer (Utah State University Press, 1992)

Cemetery and Sexton Records: A Research Guide, by Holly Hansen, James L. Tanner and Arlene H. Eakle (CreateSpace Independent Publishing Platform, 2016)

Corpses, Coffins, and Crypts: A History of Burial, by Penny Colman (Square Fish, 2015)

Death and Bereavement Across Cultures: Second edition, edited by Pittu Laungani and William Young (Routledge, 2015)

Death, Mourning, and Burial: A Cross-Cultural Reader, edited by Antonius C.G.M. Robben (Wiley-Blackwell, 2017)

Early American Gravestone Art in Photographs, by Francis Y. Duval and Ivan B. Rigby (Dover, 1978)

Early Gravestones in Southern Maine: The Genius of Bartlett Adams, by Ron Romano (The History Press, 2016)

Final Thoughts: Eternal Beauty in Stone, by John Thomas Grant (Schiffer Publishing, Ltd., 2011)

Forever Dixie: A Field Guide to Southern Cemeteries & Their Residents, by Douglas Keister (Gibbs Smith, 2008)

Going Out in Style: The Architecture of Eternity, by Douglas Keister (Checkmark Books, 1997)

Graven Images: New England Stonecarving and its Symbols, 1650–1815, by Allen Ludwig (Wesleyan, 2000)

Meet Me At Père Lachaise: a guided tour of Père Lachaise Cemetery, by Anna Eriksson (CreateSpace Independent Publishing Platform, 2010)

Memorials for Children of Change: The Art of Early New England Stonecarving, by Dickran Tashjian and Ann Tashjian (Wesleyan, 1974)

New Orleans Cemeteries: Life in the Cities of the Dead, by Robert P. Florence and J. Mason Florence (Batture Press, 2005)

Restless Peace: Images from the Cemeteries of Paris, by Stephen Sharnoff (CreateSpace Independent Publishing Platform, 2010)

Saving Graces, by David Robinson (W. W. Norton & Company, 1995)

Soul in the Stone: Cemetery Art from America's Heartland, by John Gary Brown (University Press of Kansas, 1994)

Stories in Stone: A Field Guide to Cemetery Symbolism and Iconography, by Douglas Keister (Gibbs Smith, 2004)

Stories Told In Stone: Cemetery Iconology, by Gaylord Cooper (MOTES, 2009)

The Victorian Book of the Dead, by Chris Woodyard (Kestrel Publications, 2014)

Victorian Cemetery Art, by Edmund Vincent Gillon (Dover, 1972)

Magazines

American Cemetery and Cremation
Monthly, print and digital
<www.katesboylston.com/AmericanCemetery>

Family Tree Magazine
Bi-monthly, print and digital
<www.familytreemagazine.com>

Blogs and Websites

A Grave Interest
Cemetery and genealogy history, mysteries and culture, run by this book's author. <www.agraveinterest.blogspot.com>

African American Cemeteries Online
Search for cemeteries by state, discover endangered cemeteries, and find more information on Black churches, funeral homes, and newspapers. <africanamericancemeteries.com>

Ancestry
The Internet's largest genealogy website has millions of genealogy records, including census, military, and death/burial. You'll need a paid subscription for many collections, but you can take advantage of a free two-week trial. <www.ancestry.com>

Association for Gravestone Studies
This organization further studies and preservation of gravestones through workshops, conferences, publications, and exhibits. <www.gravestonestudies.org>

BillionGraves

This website is the world's largest resource of searchable GPS cemetery data. <billiongraves.com>

Cyndi's List

Search the site for *cemetery* and discover thousands of links, from cemeteries listed by state to sites that delve into symbolism and iconology. <www.cyndislist.com/cyndislistsearch/?q=cemetery>

Exploring Almost Forgotten Gravesites in Ohio

Dedicated to cemetery preservation issues in Ohio <www.limesstones.blogspot.com>

FamilySearch

This organization, run by the Church of Jesus Christ of Latter-Day Saints, offers the world's largest collection of free family trees, genealogy records, and other resources. <www.familysearch.org>

Find A Grave

This free site is great for researching the final resting place of the famous, the infamous, and everyone else. <www.findagrave.com>

Friends of Historic Riverside Cemetery

Supporting awareness and preservation of Denver's oldest cemetery <www.friendsofriversidecemetery.org>

Granite in My Blood

Photographs of the stones of the author's ancestors and cemeteries she is transcribing <www.granite-in-my-blood.blogspot.com>

The Graveyard Detective

Looking for stories behind the graves <www.graveyarddetective.blogspot.com>

Graveyard Rabbit of Sandusky Bay

Member of the Association of Graveyard Rabbits <www.graveyardrabbitofsanduskybay.blogspot.com>

INTERMENT

Search this site's listing of millions of cemetery records from thousands of cemeteries. <www.interment.net>

The National Archives

This organization (often abbreviated as NARA) has resources for starting or continuing your family history journey. Search under "Cemetery" for a wealth of records. <www.archives.gov/research/genealogy>

National Park Service: Civil War Cemeteries

More than 620,000 soldiers killed in the Civil War are buried in fourteen national cemeteries, and you can find their locations here. Also search for soldiers by name, grave number, unit name, or location. <www.nps.gov/civilwar/search-cemeteries.htm>

National Preservation Institute

This organization offers continuing education and professional training on the management, preservation, and stewardship of cultural heritage including cemeteries. <www.npi.org>

The Peripatetic Graveyard Rabbit

Information on graveyards around the United States <www.seriousrabbit.blogspot.com>

RootsWeb

This legacy website is the oldest and largest genealogy community on the Internet, with searchable databases, mailing lists, and newsletters. <home.rootsweb.ancestry.com>

Saving Graves

This cemetery preservation alliance works to preserve and protect human burial sites from unauthorized and unwarranted disturbances by man or nature. <www.savinggraves.net>

Southern Graves

A look at Southern cemetery research <blog.southerngraves.net>

TheCemeteryClub

This site is dedicated to gravestone preservation, symbols, and genealogy. <www.thecemeteryclub.com>

United States Cemetery Project

Search this free site for headstone photos, biographies, obituaries, and old photographs. <uscemeteryproj.com>

Untangled Family Roots

Personal research, tips, and ideas <www.untangledfamilyroots.blogspot.com>

USGenWebProject

This site hosts a group of volunteers who work together to keep genealogy free on the Internet, with The Obituaries Project and The Tombstone Project that encourage cemetery transcription and photo contributions. <usgenweb.org>

WorldConnect Project

This site comprises a set of tools that allows you to upload, modify, link, and display your trees and share family genealogy with other researchers. <wc.rootsweb.ancestry.com>

World War I Cemeteries

Here you'll find a comprehensive guide to over four thousand military cemeteries and memorials throughout the world with photographs, historical information, and directions to cemeteries where WWI soldiers are buried. <www.ww1cemeteries.com>

World War II Cemeteries

Like the WWI site, you'll find photographs, historical information, and directions to cemeteries where WWII soldiers are buried. <www.ww2cemeteries.com>

E-Books and Webinars

I Seek Dead People: Tricks for Researching an Ancestor's Passing, David A. Fryxell. F+W Media <www.shopfamilytree.com/i-seek-dead-people-webinar>

Cemetery Research, by Sharon Atkins (Millennia Corporation, 2013)

Cemetery Research on the Internet (A Genealogy Guide) (One-Hour Genealogist Book 5), by Nancy Hendrickson (Green Pony Press, Inc., 2014)

Funeral Customs (Forgotten Books), by Bertram S. Puckle (Forgotten Books, 2008)

Genealogists Research Trip Planner eBook, Editors of Family Tree Magazine (F+W Media)

How to Use FindAGrave.com for Genealogy Research, by Karen Barnes (Amazon Digital Services LLC, 2013)

If the Stones Could Speak: A Guide to the Shapes and Symbols in Your Local Cemetery, by Ryland Brown (Gateway Seminars, 2014)

INDEX

ACKNOWLEDGMENTS

I would like to thank those who went above and beyond in helping me gather the necessary information and photos for this book, and for those who shouted encouragement from the sidelines. It was all much appreciated!

Deepest gratitude to Nancy McCabe, Professor of Writing and Director of the Writing Program, University of Pittsburgh at Bradford Faculty, and Creative Writing at Spalding University, for helping make it possible for me to continue pursuing my MFA at Spalding and write a book at the same time. Your editing and mentoring skills were superb.

Sincere thanks to Chris Cooke, Superintendent of Cemeteries for the City of Evansville, Indiana, for unfailing assistance in answering questions and dusting off ancient tomes in search of specific forms and records. Your cemetery is one of my favorite haunts.

Deep appreciation to Vicki Edwards, Genealogy Specialist at Pike County Public Library in Petersburg, Indiana, who dug deep in the files to tell me scandalous things I never knew about my ancestors. Your assistance was amazing.

Thank you to Richard King, Reference Librarian at Vincennes University in Vincennes, Indiana, for always being willing to lend a hand or photo when needed. You are my favorite reference librarian/accordion player.

Allen Helderman, thanks to your uncanny ability to locate forgotten files, and your great genealogy contacts. I was able to include information I didn't even know existed. Your help is always appreciated.

Brian Neighbors, you were right. (Yes, I put that in print.) "It's a mystery" how any of this gets done, but it does. You have my enduring love and thanks for your unwavering encouragement to pursue my dreams. Now, it's time for another cemetery picnic!

DEDICATION

To my husband Brian who took me to the cemetery on a date and showed me that these hallowed grounds were pretty cool places. (Of course, the picnic basket, amazing company, and bottle of wine didn't hurt.)

ABOUT THE AUTHOR

As an avowed "Tombstone Tourist," Joy Neighbors has an avid interest in cemeteries, history, photography and genealogy. She has researched and written her weekly cemetery culture blog, *A Grave Interest* <agraveinterest.blogspot.com>, for over six years, and enjoys presenting what she's learned about cemeteries and genealogy to groups and organizations around the country.

Besides cemeteries, Joy has a passion for wine. She has worked in the wine industry as a writer, winery owner, and marketing director for over 17 years. She writes a weekly wine blog called *Joy's JOY of Wine* <joysjoyofwine.blogspot.com>, and is also a wine judge and a regular wine columnist for several magazines.

Joy is pursuing her MFA in creative nonfiction at Spalding University. When she's not out "Cemetery Hopping," she "trods the boards" as a theatre actor and is a trained Improv comedian.

PHOTO CREDITS

Courtesy of Julie Barnett: title page image; images A and F in chapter 1; image M (lower) in chapter 2; chapter title image in chapter 4; images B, F, H, I (left), N, P, Q, R, T, W, and X in chapter 6

4 FREE

FAMILY TREE templates

- decorative family tree posters
- five-generation ancestor chart
- family group sheet
- bonus relationship chart
- type and save, or print and fill out

Download at <ftu.familytreemagazine.com/free-family-tree-templates

MORE GREAT GENEALOGY RESOURCES